the Eastern Caribbean

REG BUTLER

In Association with
THOMSON HOLIDAYS

1995/96

SETTLE PRESS

While every reasonable care has been taken by the author and publisher in presenting the information in this book, no responsibility can be taken by them or by Thomson Holidays for any inaccuracies. Information and prices were correct at time of printing.

Text © 1993 Reg Butler
2nd edition 1994

All rights reserved. No part of this publication may be reproduced or transmitted in any form or by any means without permission.
First published by Settle Press
10 Boyne Terrace Mews
London W11 3LR

ISBN (Paperback) 1 872876 29 3
Printed by Villiers Publications
19 Sylvan Avenue
London N3 2LE
Maps by Mary Butler

Foreword

As Britain's leading holiday company operating to the Caribbean, Thomson are happy to be associated with Reg Butler's new book 'The Key to Antigua, Barbados and St Lucia'. In writing the book, the author worked closely with experts who have year-round contact with holiday-makers' travel interests.

Whichever island you have chosen for your holiday, we feel this pocket book can act as a quick reference guide to the sightseeing potential beyond the beaches.

When the holiday is over, we suggest you keep this guide-book to help plan your return visit to one of the other islands which you didn't have time to visit.

All prices mentioned in the text were accurate at the time of printing. But each of the islands has an inflation problem, and local prices may change during the coming year. However, any costs quoted in the book can serve as guidance to the average level of expenses.

THOMSON HOLIDAYS

Contents

Page
1. **INTRODUCTION TO THE EASTERN CARIBBEAN** 2

2. **PLANNING TO GO**
   - 2.1 Which season? The weather — 11
   - 2.2 Visa and entry regulations — 11
   - 2.3 Changing money; credit cards. — 13
   - 2.4 What to pack, and what to wear — 14
   - 2.5 Health care — 15
   - 2.6 Getting married in the Caribbean — 17

3. **ANTIGUA**
   - 3.1 In the naval tradition — 19
   - 3.2 Arrival – orientation — 22
   - 3.3 At your service: money; transport, electricity — 23
   - 3.4 Places to visit — 23
   - 3.5 Take a trip — 26
   - 3.6 All the sports — 27
   - 3.7 Shopping – where and what to buy — 28
   - 3.8 Eating out — 29
   - 3.9 Nightlife — 29
   - 3.10 Quick facts — 29
   - 3.11 Festivals and Public holidays — 31
   - 3.12 Useful addresses — 32

4. **BARBADOS**
   - 4.1 The Barbados heritage — 33
   - 4.2 Arrival – orientation — 37
   - 4.3 At your service: money; transport, electricity — 38
   - 4.4 Places to visit — 40
   - 4.5 Take a trip — 48
   - 4.6 All the sports — 49
   - 4.7 Shopping – where and what to buy — 50
   - 4.8 Eating out — 51
   - 4.9 Nightlife — 53
   - 4.10 Quick facts — 54
   - 4.11 Festivals and Public holidays — 56
   - 4.12 Useful addresses — 57

5. **ST LUCIA**
   - 5.1 Jewel of the Caribbean — 59
   - 5.2 Arrival – orientation — 61
   - 5.3 At your service: money; transport, electricity — 62
   - 5.4 Places to visit — 63
   - 5.5 Take a trip — 67
   - 5.6 All the sports — 69
   - 5.7 Shopping – where and what to buy — 70
   - 5.8 Eating out — 71
   - 5.9 Nightlife — 74
   - 5.10 Quick facts — 75
   - 5.11 Festivals and Public holidays — 76
   - 5.12 Useful addresses — 77

6. ST KITTS & NEVIS
6.1	The Columbus connection	79
6.2	Arrival – orientation	81
6.3	At your service: money; transport; electricity	81
6.4	Places to visit	82
6.5	Take a trip	84
6.6	All the sports	84
6.7	Shopping – where and what to buy	85
6.8	Eating out	85
6.9	Nightlife	86
6.10	Festivals and Public holidays	86
6.11	Useful addresses	86

7. CASH CROPS AND FRUIT 87

8. CARIBBEAN EATING AND DRINKING 90

9. TRAVEL TIPS AND INFORMATION
9.1	Tipping	93
9.2	East Caribbean time	93
9.3	Phoning home	93
9.4	Newspapers, radio & TV	94
9.5	Security	95
9.6	Photo hints	95

Maps

The Windward and Leeward Islands	8
Antigua	20
Barbados – Highways & sites	34
Barbados – Parishes	35
St Lucia	60
St Kitts & Nevis	80

Chapter One

Introduction to the Eastern Caribbean

Prewar, it all started with banana boats. A select number of passengers travelled to and from the West Indies in leisured style, to escape the northern winters of Europe and America. Spacious hotels catered for clients who could afford not only money, but time.

Today's world of charter flights and scheduled services has brought the Caribbean within reach of the two-week holidaymaker. During the past decade or two, a complete tourist infrastructure has developed, with accommodation that ranges from self-catering apartments to the most luxurious of five-star hotel resorts.

The British colonial heritage helps give a special charm to St Kitts, Antigua and Barbados, while St Lucia had sufficient exposure to French influence to add a Gallic spice to the culture and cuisine. All these islands have a 20th-century political history of popular democracy and peaceful transfer of power.

A preference for unarmed bobbies, driving on the left, and a dedication to the more English-style sports are all part of the heritage which can help UK visitors feel at home.

Typical is the devotion to cricket – the national sport of the British West Indies. In legendary Vivian Richards, Antigua has produced one of the finest cricketers the game has seen, while in Barbados the big name is Sir Garfield Sobers. Every youngster's ambition is to rise to that level of fame and relative fortune. You'll see the kids playing and practising everywhere, in scratch games on the beach, on any patch of open ground or along the road.

With that enthusiastic base, through school games to club and regional first-class fixtures, it's not surprising that West Indian players dominate the world of Test cricket. When major games are played, the massed spectators are in fervent support of their heroes on the field. Even if you're not a cricket fan, it's worth attending a game to catch the West Indian flavour.

The cultural exchange is two-way. The Caribbean communities of London and New York have brought Carnival colour to London's Notting Hill during the

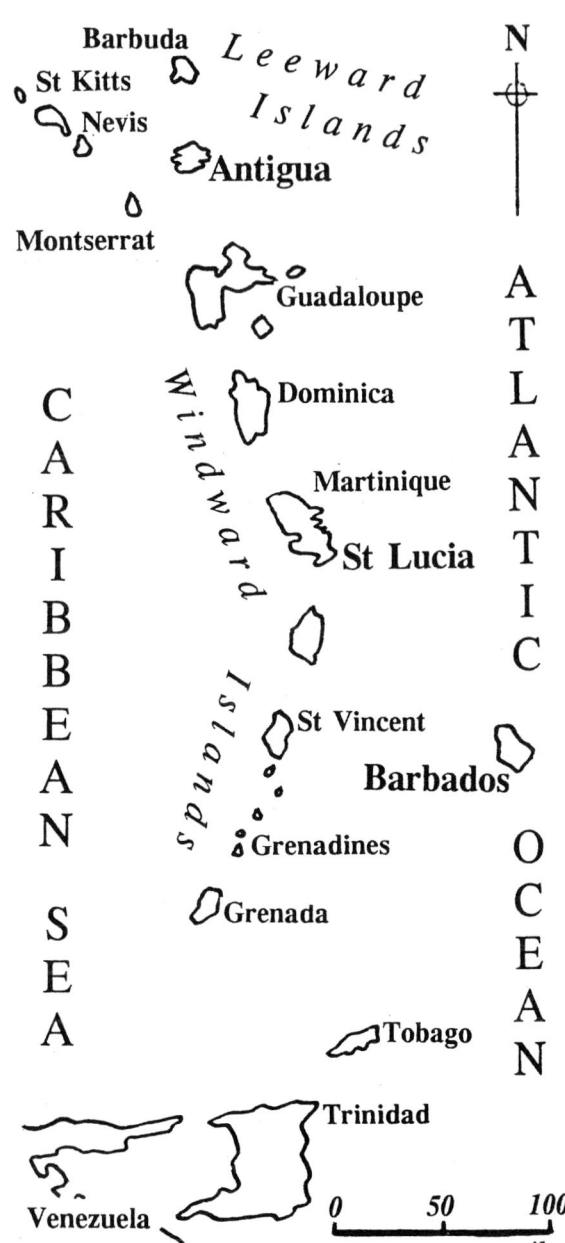

August Bank Holiday, or to Brooklyn's Eastern Parkway on Labor Day.

Each island has its ethnic Carnival, when visitors can enjoy the home version of those stunning parades. The palate twitches to the aroma of curried goat and barbecued chicken, while revellers in their dazzling costumes strut to the infectious rhythms of reggae and calypso.

Whether your choice is Antigua, St Kitts, Barbados or St Lucia, there's ample local colour any time of the year, as a bonus to the beach life of sand, warm sea and rustling palm trees.

Everywhere there are friendly faces. Music and dance have an enormous influence on West Indian life. In streets, restaurants and bars there is a permanent flow of Caribbean music, recorded or live.

For the historically or cultural-minded visitor, there is plenty to see and do beyond the manicured hotel beaches – from exploring the wilder shores of the rugged Atlantic coastlines to more tranquil walks through idyllic tropical gardens.

With a hired vehicle or on a sightseeing tour by minibus or boat, it's possible to reach deserted beaches and sparkling bays, backed by a dense growth of coconut palms and other tropical trees which would make Robinson Crusoe feel in his element.

Each island has its individual natural beauty, with luxuriant forests, and banana or sugar-cane or pineapple plantations. Geologically, the islands are built mostly on a foundation of coral rock, overlaid with limestone. These formations ensure a very pure water supply. The vegetation is fascinating to visitors from other climatic zones. Wayside plants and trees are a gardener's delight in these lands of lush fertility.

Of course, most visitors come mainly for the beaches, water-sports and relaxed living of the principal resorts. For the sport-minded, there's every available facility from tennis to volleyball, ping-pong and golf.

The all-inclusive concept has taken off in all four islands, following the success of the idea in other Carribean destinations. Briefly, the provision of a 'totally all-inclusive holiday for an all-inclusive price' is a further development from 'full board' or 'American Plan'. To mark the change, many hotels describe themselves as 'clubs' or 'resorts'. You pay one package price, and the rest is taken care of.

Each establishment features its distinctive style of amenities and dining options, land and water sports. Devotees have every facility for water-skiing, sailing, wind-surfing and scuba-diving.

Arrangements vary. Some hotels offer one hour free every day for wind-surfing, snorkelling and sail-boating. Any other sports like banana boat, scuba-diving and water-skiing, you pay direct at the water-sport centre. Tariffs are often listed in US dollars, but you can pay in local currency.

The all-inclusive concept can even extend to the provision of unlimited local drinks throughout the day. The measures are generous: Caribbean rum-based cocktails, draught beer, fruit juices, table wine or even Californian bubbly.

From breakfast till past midnight there is choice of full programmes of in-house sport activities and entertainment. But there's no chivvying of guests who prefer to concentrate on their suntan around the pool, keeping thirst at bay with a rum punch.

With virtually everything provided, some holidaymakers are reluctant to stir past their club entrance gate. But outside is the workaday West Indies, which also has great fascination. It's a pity to come so far, without getting closer to the Caribbean experience. Hopefully this booklet will encourage a Columbus spirit, to get out and explore.

Chapter Two

Planning to go

2.1 Which season?

All four islands offer a very steady year-round temperature that averages in the eighties Fahrenheit. Likewise the daily hours of sunshine hold steady between six and seven hours in the rain-clouded summer months, to nine or even ten hours in the drier winter season.

June to November are the months of heaviest rainfall – typically tropical, in buckets but of short duration. After a daytime downpour, the sun rapidly reappears and everything soon dries out. Rain need not wreck your day.

Antigua is one of the driest Caribbean islands – average 45 inches a year – and is therefore not as lush as islands like St Lucia. The pleasant, tropical climate is warm throughout the year. Neighbouring St Kitts & Nevis follow an identical pattern.

Barbados has a similar sub-tropical climate with 3000 hours of sunshine per annum. Annual average temperature is 80 degrees F. A gentle sea breeze alleviates even the hottest days.

In St Lucia the deluges of rain are usually brief and refreshing though most frequent in June or July. Winter temperatures range between 65 minimum and 85 maximum.

June through October is the prime season for Caribbean hurricanes, with September the most likely. Resort hotels are solidly built to cope.

2.2 Visa and entry formalities

A full and valid passport and a return or onward ticket is required by all persons entering any of the islands. Passports should be valid for six months after the planned date of return. No-passport entry is possible for US and Canadian citizens who are visiting for not more than six months. They can enter on production of proof of citizenship such as a birth certificate. Visas are not required for citizens of Britain, USA, the Commonwealth or of most West European countries.

Before landing, passengers are given an immigration form to fill out. The immigration official gives it a quick

MAX – Average monthly maximum temperatures – °F.
SUN – Average daily hours of sunshine.
RAIN – Average monthly rainfall in inches.
HUMID – Average monthly percentage humidity.

	J	F	M	A	M	J	J	A	S	O	N	D	Annual rainfall
ANTIGUA													
Max	82	83	83	85	86	86	87	87	88	87	85	84	
Sun	8	8	8	8	7.5	8	8	7	6	7	7	7	
Rain	3	2	2	3	4	4	5	5	6	6	5.5	5	50.5"
Humid	67	63	62	60	61	64	65	67	67	67	69	68	
BARBADOS													
Max	84	86	86	88	88	88	88	88	88	88	86	84	
Sun	10	10	9	8	7	7	7	8	8	7	8	9	
Rain	2.0	1.0	1.0	1.5	2.0	4.0	5.0	6.0	6.5	6.5	7.0	3.0	45.5"
Humid	71	66	64	65	67	70	71	72	73	76	78	73	
ST. LUCIA													
Max	83	83	84	87	88	88	87	88	88	97	85	83	
Sun	9	9	8	8	7	6	7	8	7	8	8	8	
Rain	5.3	3.6	3.8	3.4	5.9	8.6	9.3	10.5	9.9	9.3	9.1	7.8	86.5"
Humid	70	68	65	64	65	69	71	69	70	69	75	71	

glance, and you're through. Luggage trolleys are available as far as the customs desks, and porters can assist. Duty free allowances into each of the islands is standardised at 200 cigarettes or 50 cigars or 250 grammes of tobacco; and one litre of either spirits or wine.

At the exit from customs, you are met by tour reps who escort you for transfer to your hotel. Independent travellers will normally find taxis awaiting at the airport. Before accepting any offers of transport, ask the Information Desk for guidance on what standard price to pay. Like the world over, airport cabbies are renowned for scalping the innocent.

Looking ahead to final departure, an exit tax of US $10 is levied by Antigua and St Lucia, US$8 by St Kitts & Nevis, or $12.50 by Barbados. Tour operators such as Thomson Holidays include these charges in the cost of the holiday package, and pay them on their clients' behalf. Other travellers should be prepared.

2.3 Money

Currencies of all four islands are linked to the US dollar. Antigua, St Lucia and St Kitts & Nevis use the East Caribbean dollar, fixed at the time of printing this book at $2.70 EC to one US dollar. The Barbados dollar is fixed at two Barbados for one US.

Depending on the cross-rate between US dollars and sterling, the local island currencies fluctuate against the pound. In practice, you'll always get the best rate with US dollars, and it's advisable to travel with US dollar cheques and banknotes, rather than sterling or any other hard currency.

Currency can be changed into the local island dollars at airport booths and commercial banks. Hotels give a lower rate of exchange. You cannot use Eurocheques.

There are no restrictions on the import or export of the local currencies. At the end of your stay, any remaining cash can be re-exchanged. But it's good strategy to spend up your local dollars, just keeping some in reserve for a final drink at the airport.

Major credit cards (Visa, Access/Mastercard, American Express) are widely accepted by restaurants, hotels and duty free shops, and also in payment of car hire and sightseeing tours.

Caution: a charge of 5% is normally made on credit card transactions. That applies to any purchases made with plastic, where the price is loaded by that percentage. Check whether payment by cash or traveller cheques may be more advantageous.

Often prices are quoted in US dollars, and are then converted into local dollars. Especially when negotiating with cabbies and other fast operators, be completely clear which brand of dollars is being agreed.

2.4 What to wear and pack

The Caribbean can be hot and humid, so beach and lightweight casual clothing is the order of the day. Bring both bits of bikini, as topless is not acceptable at most resorts. Shorts and beachwear should not be worn in town. Islanders are wonderfully courteous but they consider that swim suits and see-throughs are strictly for the beach. Pack cover-ups for shopping trips, excursions or snacks at the bar.

Evenings tend to be smarter, but still casual, though many hotels ask gentlemen to wear long trousers at dinner. Light-weight suits and dresses, and casual loose fitting cotton clothes are ideal. But take a light sweater for the chill of air-conditioned restaurants, or for winter evenings.

Some hotels and casinos require jacket and tie at night, or on special occasions. Depending on the chosen hotel, casual elegance with a touch of glamour sums up the evening scene. For men, a dinner jacket may be needed for gala events.

Laundry service is available in most hotels. Simply leave a message for the maid and allow 24/48 hours for laundering. You can expect to pay around £2 per shirt and £3 per dress.

Most hotels provide towels for use by the pool, or there may be a small charge. But consider packing a couple of beach towels for sampling other beaches.

If you intend to do any exploring on foot, the terrain may be quite rough; so bring a comfortable and sturdy pair of shoes. Likewise, pack any personal equipment you may need for sport activities: a hard hat for horse-riding; snorkelling gear; or a helmet if you intend to rent a scooter.

During summer, unexpected downpours of rain can be very refreshing, and quite enjoyable if you are ready equipped with a plastic mac or an umbrella. Equally useful is a hat to keep the sun at bay.

Don't forget suntan lotion, toiletries and any medicines which you take regularly. Even if your favourite brands are available in the islands, they'll certainly be more expensive than back home. Insect repellents can be a blessing.

A final reminder: bring plenty of film and a supply of reading matter. Photo supplies and books are more expensive than back home.

2.5 Health care

Jabs

No vaccination certificates are required. Some medical people lean heavily towards ultra-caution, and recommend a full range of inoculations against Typhoid, Polio, Tetanus and Hepatitis A. Others suggest that these precautions are not essential if you are taking normal care of yourself, and not visiting any outlandish areas. The Caribbean islands are rated as a low-risk area, with no malaria, typhoid, dysentery or any of those horrors. However, ask your own doctor's advice at least four weeks before departure. For further details on health requirements contact the Hospital for Tropical Diseases Healthline on 0839 337 722. Code number 23.

Mosquitoes

Have your defences ready against mosquitoes, which come in 57 varieties. Mosquitoes and sand flies bite especially at dusk when they are hungry for supper. They are very partial to holidaymakers. It's wise to be frugal in use of perfumes and aftershaves, as these seem to attract them. Insect repellents are sold at chemists and in hotel-resort shops.

An excellent mosquito deterrent is (believe-it-or-not) Avon's "Skin-so-soft" bath oil spray. It's highly effective. Even sand-flies will keep their distance.

For a peaceful night's sleep, keep your windows closed after dark, and have any mosquito screens in place. Leave the air conditioner switched on.

Sun and health

Deep suntan is often regarded as a sign of health, but doctors advise caution against overdoing it, because of skin-cancer risk. To avoid sunburn, the standard advice is well enough known. But many holidaymakers don't fully realise the power of the tropical sun, which can still burn even if you are sitting in the shade, where bright sunshine can be reflected off water or sand. Ultraviolet rays can also strike through clouds, though a heavy overcast sky does offer some protection.

When working on your suntan, go easy for the first few days. Take the sun in very small doses and wear a wide-brimmed sun hat, or a baseball-type cap. Take extra care whenever your shadow is shorter than your height. The shorter your shadow, the more risk of sunburn. Avoid the UV danger time between noon and 2 p.m. Resume your sunbathing late afternoon when the sun is not so strong.

Use plenty of high-factor suntan lotion – SPF of 15 or over – reapplied every hour or so after you've been in the pool. Wear a T-shirt while swimming or snorkelling. If your exposed skin has turned pink or red by evening, be more careful next day!

Hopefully you'll go home with a tan that's golden and not lobster red or peeling. Be cautious about beachside hair-braiding services which expose strips of your scalp to the sun. Wear a head covering. It's no fun to get a sunburnt scalp.

In case of heatstroke – marked by headache, flushed skin and high temperature – get medical advice. Meanwhile wrap yourself in wet towels, and drink fruit juice or water.

Finally, beware of iced drinks while sunbathing, and then jumping in the pool. Your tummy is bound to rebel.

Water

Tap water can be drunk anywhere. There's certainly nothing to worry about in the drinks and ice cubes served in hotels and restaurants. However, bottled purified and mineral water is also available. In Antigua the mains water is chlorinated, and may cause some stomachs to protest until accustomed to the flavour.

Stomach upsets

Most upsets are caused by unaccustomed food, very cold drinks and hot sun. If you're not accustomed to quantities of fresh fruit, go easy at first with all that tempting tropical produce. Give your stomach time to attune itself to a deluge of pineapple juice, piña coladas, and fruit punches. Be wary about down-market local restaurants, where kitchen standards may be less than ideal.

If you want to come prepared, bring pharmaceuticals such as Lomotil, Imodium or Arrêt, which are usually effective.

Imodium can be bought at any UK chemists.

Usually the problem takes 24 hours to clear up. If your stomach is still complaining after a couple of days, see a doctor. There's no point in suffering. He'll fix you with tablets or an injection.

Warnings!

Snorkellers especially should beware of the spiny sea urchins in shallow water reefs along the shore. They are very painful if touched or stood upon, when the spines break off in your skin. Don't try to dig them out. Apply antiseptic, and they will finally dissolve.

Do not touch the fruit of the Manchineel tree which abounds along many beaches. The small green fruit, which resembles a crab apple, is poisonous if eaten, and can cause serious blistering if touched. Even the bark and leaves are extremely toxic.

The tree has now been eliminated from most hotel beaches but may still be found on secluded beaches. The fruit produces a poisonous sap and blistering can occur if you rub against it. The tree should not be used as a shelter from the rain, as even the drips can blister. Many Manchineel trees are clearly labelled, or painted with a red ring.

There are a few poisonous snakes in St Lucia, but they are found in the interior and hardly ever encountered by tourists.

You will probably see cockroaches. Although off-putting, they are harmless and do not reflect the standard of cleanliness.

Swimmers should beware the undertow on the Atlantic side of the islands.

Finally, a reminder to scuba divers: avoid diving during one or two days before flying. The pressurisation of airline cabins can entail a dangerous risk of "the bends".

2.6 Getting married in the Caribbean

Sunkissed beaches, lush scenery and year-round tropical sunshine have made the Caribbean a runaway best-seller in the weddings and honeymoon market.

Romance is now big business, more popular than ever among newly-weds and those poised to tie the knot. The islands boast dozens of exotic hotels designed with couples in mind, ranging from lively resorts to secluded hideaways.

True romantics planning a Caribbean wedding have a choice of tailor-made settings for their nuptials ranging from garlanded gazebos with hummingbirds darting among the scented flowers, to luxury yachts and palm-fringed beaches. The ceremony can be as simple or lavish as they choose - whether it's a grand event with all the trimmings or a barefoot ceremony in the sand.

The Caribbean also offers excellent value for money, with a choice of accommodation to suit all pockets. Weddings are organized at a very reasonable add-on cost to the normal holiday honeymoon package – or even gratis, except for a modest arrangement fee.

Couples can thus marry in a location that's far more romantic and memorable than the average Registry Office, but also dramatically cut the cost of their wedding.

Virtually every luxury property in the Caribbean now targets honeymooners. Many hotels offer extras ranging from complimentary room upgrades to free bubbly, flowers and breakfast in bed next morning. Some employ full-time wedding co-ordinators who will arrange every detail of the big day, discussing each couple's needs and requirements individually.

Obviously, advance planning is necessary. All the arrangements can be made through a specialist department of the tour operator. Thomson Holidays, for instance, produce a special Weddings in Paradise brochure with world-wide options.

Original Documents

Depending on which island is chosen for the ceremony, here's a check-list of the essential documents to be produced in person before the local Registrar (foreign documents must be translated officially into English):

- Passport and Birth Certificate;
- If one of the parties is a divorcee, proof of Decree Absolute is required;
- In the case of a widow/widower, a Death Certificate of the first spouse is required;
- If a name has been changed by Deed Poll, proof is required;
- Evidence of parental consent if one of the parties is under age of 18;
- Proof of single status in the form of a statutory declaration stamped and signed by a solicitor.

Residency

Bride and groom must be on the island several working days before the ceremony can be performed: Antigua 3 working days, St Lucia 7 days, Barbados 6 days, St Kitts & Nevis 2 days.

Chapter Three

Antigua

3.1 In the naval tradition

The largest of the Leeward Islands, Antigua (pronounced An-*tee*-ga) sits just north of Guadeloupe with its smaller sister island, Barbuda, close by. Blessed almost year-round with an ideal climate, Antigua offers a choice of 365 powdery white sand beaches. Anyone demanding a different beach for every day of the year could always do a day trip to Barbuda in a Leap Year.

Visitors can choose from over 40 hotels. Whether it's a luxury hotel conveniently located near St. John's, a charming historic inn with a harbour view, or an exclusive resort on its own tiny island reached by a private launch, visitors will find accommodation well suited to their needs.

Many people just want to relax and unwind. But Antigua can also offer a full range of land and water sport facilities. Antigua claims rank as the sailing capital of the Leeward Islands, and each year hosts a prestigious international regatta based on Nelson's Dockyard at English Harbour.

Most hotels offer a variety of sail craft for hire, with or without crew, for pleasure boating around the coast. There are also extensive offshore reefs and accessible wrecks for scuba divers. Other watersport facilities include windsurfing, snorkelling, water skiing, jet skiing, parasailing and deep sea fishing.

For history buffs, the island has a selection of historic sights and attractions, mainly related to the period when Antigua was the naval base for Britain's control of the Caribbean colonies.

The island was originally inhabited in stone age times by the Siboney tribe, who arrived from North America. Some 2,000 years later, around the time of Christ, the island was occupied by Arawak Indians, a peaceful and industrious group from South America who called their home Waladli. The much fiercer Caribs took over around 1200 AD.

Christopher Columbus discovered the island in 1493 during his second voyage to the New World. He named the island after a greatly revered statue of the Virgin –

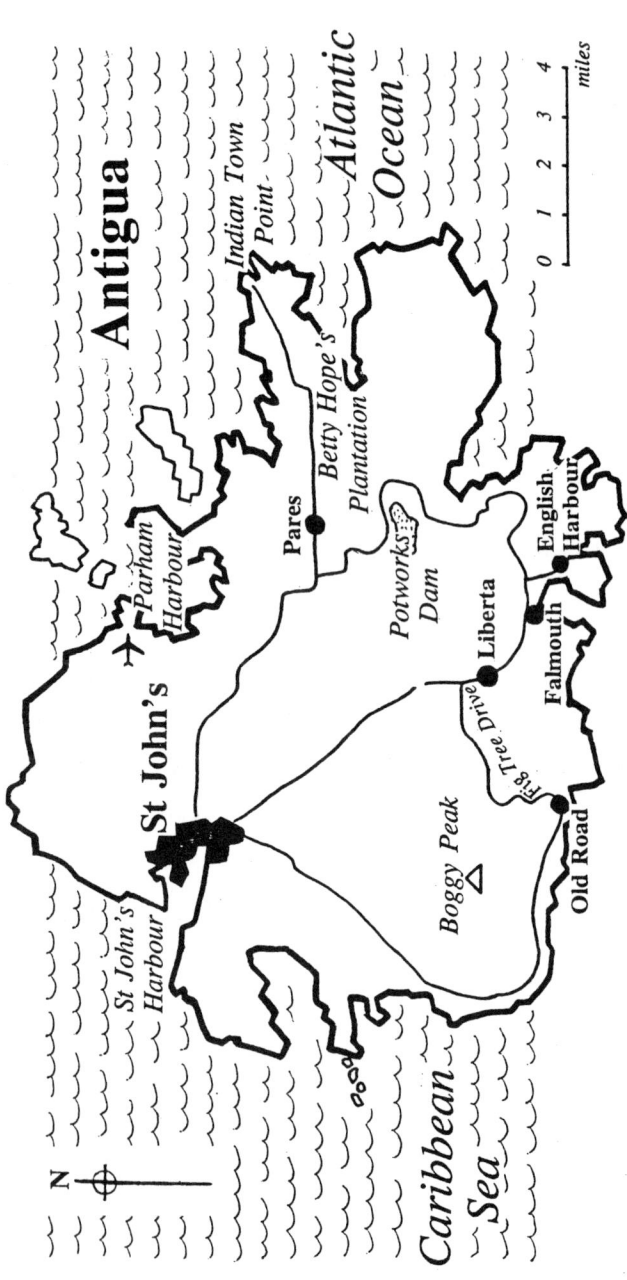

Santa Maria de la Antigua – in a chapel of Seville Cathedral where Columbus prayed before starting on a new journey.

Not much happened for the next 140 years, except for a few sporadic attempts at settlement by the Spaniards and French, who were discouraged by Carib resistance and the lack of fresh water.

In 1632, Antigua was occupied by a group of English settlers from neighbouring St Kitts. The early economy was devoted to tobacco production. That was abandoned from 1674 in favour of sugar, introduced from Barbados by Christopher Codrington. In parallel with other Caribbean islands, the plantations required a massive import of African slaves: hence the predominant make-up of the present population.

Sugar brought great prosperity to the planters. By the early 19th century, around 160 estates each had its grandiose Plantation House, and a stone windmill for grinding the cane. But the grandeur faded during the 19th century, when cheaper sugar was produced elsewhere and the slaves were freed in 1834.

Meanwhile Antigua had been chosen as Britain's naval bastion in the West Indies, using English Harbour as a heavily fortified base. The coastline bristled with forts and defence systems, and the French and Spaniards wisely kept their distance from this Gibraltar of the Caribbean.

There are exotic legends of beautiful Carib women falling for British officers (and vice versa with the officers' wives and the Carib men) resulting in numerous blood feuds and betrayals. One 17th century British governor rejected his wife after she had spent two years in Carib captivity! However, by the late 18th century the Caribs had disappeared as a separate ethnic group.

The most legendary name in Antiguan history was Nelson, who arrived in 1784, aged 26, as captain of *HMS Boreas* and second in command of the naval base. His three-year residence is marked today by extensive restoration which has converted Nelson's Dockyard and its surroundings into something of a Nelson industry, with a constant flow of visitors to this prime sightseeing highlight of Antigua.

During the 20th century, the sugar industry has totally disappeared, to be replaced by a sweeter harvest from the international holiday industry, based on powdery white sand instead of granulated white sugar.

After more than 300 years as a British Colony, in 1967 Antigua became the first of the Eastern Caribbean countries to attain internal self government as a State in association with Great Britain. Full independence came on November 1, 1981.

Today's democracy is run much along British lines, with a Prime Minister and Cabinet, and elections every five years. It's a peaceful place where travellers from UK will feel at home, speaking English, driving on the left, stopping for a drink at a local pub, eating a 'Nelson's sandwich' in a tea room, or watching a test match.

But it's still worth trying to master the local dialect or sampling curried conch, breadfruit, sweet potato, excellent fish dishes and the renowned sweet Antigua pineapple.

3.2 Arrival, and orientation

Getting there

British Airways flies direct from London; Britannia from London Gatwick; BWIA direct from London, New York, Miami and Toronto; charter flights by Airtours from Manchester airport; Air Canada direct from Toronto; American Airlines from JFK, New York; Lufthansa direct from Frankfurt. Flying time is approximately 8 hours from Europe; $3^1/_2$ hours from New York; 2 hours from Miami; and $4^1/_2$ hours from Toronto. The local airline called LIAT (short for the original name of Leeward Islands Air Transport) flies inter-island. It is jointly owned by 11 Caribbean governments, with HQ in Antigua.

V.C. Bird International Airport – named after the Antiguan prime minister – accommodates the largest aircraft, and features a new and modern terminal building.

Antigua is a port of call for numerous cruise ships, and has recently completed a cruise ship terminal in St John's Harbour, adjacent to the Heritage Quay duty-free shopping centre.

Arrival procedures at the airport are very straightforward. Tour representatives await as you come through customs. Thomson clients will be met by their local agent, Antours, who arrange the hotel transfers. Antours' reps will be wearing a mustard, gold and white uniform and will have a Thomson sign. For go-it-alone travellers there are plentiful taxis, with official rates for most destinations posted in the customs area.

Orientation

Antigua covers 108 square miles. The capital is St John's, a deepwater port four miles southwest of the airport. A limestone and coral island with some higher volcanic areas, Antigua is roughly circular and ringed by jagged coves, bays, and small harbours. Visitors to the southern part of the island will find lush, green hills, and can enjoy a spectacular view from Boggy Peak (1,330 feet).

Barbuda, its smaller sister island, lies about 27 miles northeast of Antigua and can be reached in 20 minutes by air. It covers 62 square miles, has a good deal of game, and is known for its pink sand beaches.

3.3 At your service

Money: Antigua uses the Eastern Caribbean dollar, also known as the "EC" or the Bee Wee Dollar, which is tied to the US dollar at an average exchange rate of $2.60 EC for $1.00 US. For the sterling equivalent, multiply $2.60 EC by the US dollar/sterling exchange rate. Thus, when it's US$1.50 to the pound, there should be around $3.90 EC to £1. Check the maths from the local newspaper. The exact rates vary at different exchange outlets.

Antiguan banking hours are daily 8.00 am – 1.00 pm, with an additional 3.00 – 5.00 pm on Fridays. Closed Saturdays.

Most prices are quoted in both US and EC dollars, and it's better to arrive with US dollar cash and traveller cheques rather than sterling.

American Express is the official credit card for Antigua, is widely accepted and there is no surcharge levied for its use. Most hotels and some restaurants and stores also accept Diners Club, Visa, Access and Mastercard, although these may be subject to a small surcharge.

Transport: A local bus service operates at a nominal fare. Taxis are marked with the letter H on a green number plate. They are unmetered, but rates for all journeys are fixed by the government. Listed prices of standard journeys are readily available. Check the rate before beginning your journey and arrange a return pick-up time for the end of an evening out.

Car hire rentals can be arranged in advance of arrival on the island. Tariffs are £25 upwards per day, with unlimited mileage but excluding fuel. A valid drivers' licence will secure a temporary visitor's permit, costing about US$12 or £8 sterling. Driving is British style, on the left.

Electricity: Dual voltage is available in most major hotels, 220 AC, 50 cycles; and 110 AC, 60 cycles. Plugs are American type, 2 pin. If you are travelling with electric appliances, bring a plug adaptor – available in department stores and at the departure airport.

3.4 Places to visit

Antigua's colonial legacy is most evident in the well-preserved attractions located throughout the island, especially the old fortifications. Disused windmills that used to service the sugar plantations dot the plains and rolling hillsides. The two major points of interest are the capital city of St. John's on the northwestern side of the island and English Harbour on the south side.

St John's

The capital of Antigua is the focal point of the highway system, and the principal market centre. The town's

36,000 residents represent more than half the island's population. Pastel-coloured shops and houses line the streets, which are a delight to explore on foot. A grid pattern to the central area, and a one-way traffic system, makes life easier for the pedestrian.

The Anglican **St John's Cathedral** is a favourite photo subject. The church was founded in 1683 but was replaced by a stone building in 1745, which in turn was destroyed by an earthquake almost a century later. From 1845 the present cathedral was rebuilt. The figures of St John the Baptist and St John the Divine at the south gate were supposedly taken from one of Napoleon's ships and brought to the island by a British man-of-war.

On the corner of Long and Market Streets, the former **Old Court House**, dated 1747, is St John's oldest building. It's now used as the **Museum of Antigua and Barbuda**, with displays of historic interest, including a cricket bat used by Viv Richards. The national archives are also kept here.

The area of **Redcliffe Quay** was first used as a slave compound, and was converted into warehouses after emancipation in 1834. The waterfront zone has been pleasantly restored to form a complex of quality shops and restaurants. **Heritage Quay** is a new development likewise dedicated to up-market shopping, with Casino nightlife.

Fort James at the entrance of St. John's harbour was part of the initial defence system of 1675, but most of the present structure dates from 1749. The ten cannons have never been fired in anger.

The **Antigua Recreation Ground** is the attractive venue for major games of cricket, when the boisterous spectators are themselves part of the day's entertainment. In late July and into August, the grounds are transformed into **Carnival City**, with bands and calypso singers' performing during the run-up to the main event.

In the centre of the island, east and south-east from St John's and past the village of Pares, signs point the way to **Betty's Hope Estate**, founded by Christopher Codrington in 1674 and named after his daughter. The remains of this pioneer sugar plantation, including two windmill towers, are currently under restoration.

Still further east is **Indian Town**, one of Antigua's national parks, located at the northeastern tip of the island. Breakers roaring in with the full force of the Atlantic have created blowholes which foam with surf and spray. At the mouth of Indian Creek, a natural limestone arch called **Devil's Bridge** is a popular tourist sight. The area has yielded archaeological evidence of pre-Columbian settlement by the Arawak and Carib Indians.

In the centre of the island is **Potworks Dam Reservoir**, a man-made lake with a capacity of one billion gallons.

English Harbour

The 18th-century naval base was commissioned by the British in 1755 for the protection of its colonies when the French, Dutch and Spanish were seeking to enlarge their Caribbean possessions. Heavy fortifications were erected on **Shirley Heights**, named after the former Governor of the Leeward Islands, Sir Thomas Shirley. The gun platforms command spectacular views over the harbour from 500 feet up. Call at the **Dow's Hill Interpretation Centre** for a multi-media journey through Antigua's history. A visit takes about one hour and costs $10 EC. Archaeologists have found Carib and Arawak artifacts in this area.

Another hillside location above the dockyard is taken by **Clarence House**, which was built for Prince William Henry, the Duke of Clarence. The Prince served under Nelson's command, and later became King William 1V. Today, the house is used by the Governor, but is open to visitors when he is not in residence. Princess Margaret and Lord Snowdon honeymooned here in 1960.

The naval dockyard, now known as **Nelson's Dockyard**, began operating in 1743, and grew over the next 60 years with the development of English Harbour as a major base. Bricks used in the buildings came from England as ship's ballast. Many historical sites have been restored within the entire complex, which now has National Park status and protection. The Dockyard itself served as the headquarters for Horatio Nelson during his 3-year posting. Admirals Rodney and Hood also served here.

The harbour sheltered English warships in the West Indies until 1889. By then, battleships had become too big for the harbour, and the base was abandoned. Until the 1950's, when the whole area was restored, the dockyard was derelict. Now, recapturing something of the atmosphere of Nelson's day, the docks and museum are delightful for an afternoon stroll. They are beautifully illuminated at night for Sound and Light shows. Have lunch or a drink at the **Admiral's Inn**, which in Nelson's day was a storehouse for pitch and tar. A museum is housed in **The Admiral's House**, which was built 50 years after Nelson died. A small market sells local souvenirs and brightly coloured T-shirts.

English Harbour today is Antigua's most active yachting centre, with another popular anchorage in the neighbouring bay called **Falmouth Harbour**.

Antigua's finest scenic route is **Fig Tree Drive** between Old Road on Carlisle Bay and Liberta in the parish of St Paul. It follows a spectacular winding course through the rain forest of the hilliest part of the island and past tiny villages and the remains of old sugar mills. The trip can be combined with a scenic drive along the southwest coast with its picturesque fishing villages. An all-day tour could also include sightseeing of English Harbour.

3.5 Take a trip

Although most visitors come to Antigua to relax and sunbathe, the island also offers interesting excursions and sightseeing. There is rich and colourful birdlife, while offshore is a good range of underwater sightseeing, with splendid tropical fish and coral to view by glass-bottom boat or snorkel.

For land excursions, most taxi drivers are well versed in the island's history and in the major sights and attractions. Thanks to a continuing programme of training, the cabbies can provide a selection of half-day and whole-day circuits.

Excursions can be arranged through the Antours agency. Ask for the current price list. The prime circuit is to English Harbour and Nelson's Dockyard, with an itinerary that includes Fig Tree Drive. Half-day shopping tours to St John's are another popular option.

The Tropikelly agency specialises in off-trail tours aboard 4-wheel-drive vehicles.

Jolly Roger Cruise – A lively day or evening aboard a Pirate Ship with a barbecue meal, open bar and entertainment. The ranson money is around US$50. You can dance on the poop deck, swing on ropes, walk the plank or go snorkelling over a wreck. The two-masted schooner was the last wooden sailing ship built for the Swedish Navy, and has sailed around the world three times. It is fully equipped with cannons, skull and crossbones flag and enough barrels of rum punch to ensure that the ship never runs dry.

Glass Bottom Boats – A half day trip allows you to marvel at the underwater world off Antigua's beaches without getting your feet wet. If you'd like a closer look, take along your flippers and snorkel. Depending on the routing, there may be a chance of seeing pelicans on Pelican Island. Approx cost is £13 or US$20.

An excursion to **Great Bird Island** can be made from Dickenson Bay, with transport in glass bottom boats for a leisurely view of the reef. A 100-ft limestone cliff is an ideal habitat for nesting sea-birds.

Other islands

It is also possible to visit the nearby islands of Barbuda, Dominica, Montserrat, or St Kitts & Nevis. They are just a short flight away by LIAT, the locally-based Caribbean airline, or by independent charter. Day tour prices range from US$120 to $150, including guided tour and lunch. Everything is pre-arranged, to ensure a hassle-free day that packs in the maximum variety and interest.

Antigua's sister island of **Barbuda** is inhabited mainly by descendants of slaves brought there by the Codrington family who leased the island from the British government for 200 years, at a peppercorn rent of one fat sheep. The lease ran out in 1870. The island was then administered as a Crown Estate from 1903 until 1976, when Barbuda became virtually self-governing.

Most of the 1,200 residents live in Codrington Village. Otherwise Barbuda could double as a Robinson Crusoe island, with deserted beaches of pink coral sand, plentiful fish along the coral reefs that make access dangerous along three sides of the coastline, and some wild pigs and deer. A bird sanctuary near the airstrip is a habitat for thousands of frigate birds.

Horseback riding, snorkelling or scuba diving around shipwrecks, and hunting (wild boar, deer, duck, guinea fowl and pigeon) are among the activities available.

3.6 All the sports

Many hotels have superb **tennis** facilities, including floodlit courts for night play. Some offer tennis packages that include court time and professional instruction. Enthusiasts will know that professionals descend on Antigua for the 'Tennis Weeks' in January and April, both for competition and to train for the international tennis circuit.

Golf Cedar Valley Golf Course, a spectacular 18-hole, par 70 course, is open to the public. Equipment can be rented. Typical costs are: green fees US$20; golf cart $25; club hire $10. Every year, usually over the first weekend in August, the Pro/Am Golf Tournament is held.

There is also a 9-hole course at Half Moon Bay.

Squash is played at the Bucket Club on temporary membership.

Water sport facilities are normally featured by the resort hotels, including windsurfing, water-skiing and sunfish sailing. Scuba diving is easily arranged, and snorkelling equipment can be hired. Those who enjoy exploring the subaqua world will be enthralled by the coral reefs, lobsters and multi-coloured fish that characterise the Antiguan waters.

Scuba training courses are readily available. A typical PADI certification course would cost around US$165, including 8 hours classroom instruction and 8 hours in the pool. For certification dives, including 4 boat dives, reckon US$210.

Along the south-west coast is Cades Reef, stretching for over two miles, with abundant fish life, a wide variety of soft and hard coral, and excellent visibility. At the Ariadne Shoal, with depths ranging from 50 to 80 ft, the reefs are alive with lobster, turtles and nurse sharks. At the entrance to Deep Bay is the Andes Wreck, an 80-year-old freighter lying in 20 ft of water. This wreck is now overgrown with coral, and is home to large reef fish.

Swimming is excellent off most of the beaches and all are open to the public. The sea water is clear as gin, always at warm bath temperature. But be careful of the eastern, Atlantic coast where the sea can be choppy in places.

Antigua offers spectacular sailing and is famous for its international sailing regatta held annually during April or May. In more relaxed style, a boat opens up access to secluded coves and sheltered beaches for a day of utter tranquility. All kinds and sizes of yacht can be chartered.

Deep sea fishing can also be arranged. An annual Sportfishing Tournament is held at the end of April – early May. The record fish for the tournament has been a 25 kg kingfish. For the non-competitor there is excellent year round fishing for wahoo, kingfish, mackerel, dorado, tuna and barracuda.

Among the spectator sports, **cricket** is played everywhere in Antigua. Test Matches and other major fixtures take place at the Recreation Grounds in St John's. At a more basic level, you can often see a knockabout game with bat and ball on street corners, in playgrounds, or along the beach.

Horse races are held on public holidays at Cassada Gardens.

3.7 Shopping

Shops are closed on Thursday afternoons but are otherwise open 8-12 and 13-16 hrs Monday to Saturday. There are small stores in the villages but the larger supermarkets are in St John's. Post Office hours are 8.15-12 and 13-16 on Monday to Thursday; open until 17 hrs on Friday.

The capital of St John's offers an interesting variety of richly stocked stores and boutiques. Special purchases include local rum, straw goods, pottery, batik and silk-screened fabrics, and jewellery incorporating semi-precious Antiguan stones. China, crystal, cameras, watches and perfume are obtainable at duty-free prices.

Heritage Quay, a cruise ship pier, offers a wide variety of duty-free shops, a casino and a hotel. **Redcliffe Quay**, a restored arsenal, now houses shops and restaurants.

The colourful fruit and vegetable market each Friday and Saturday is well worth a visit.

3.8 Eating out

Good eating is a way of life in Antigua. Restaurant menus cover a range from the national cuisines of America, Europe and the Orient, fast food through to Nouvelle Cuisine. But many restaurants and hotel buffets also offer typical island dishes such as souse, ducana and salt fish, pepper pot or conch stew. Look out for 'different' items like paw-paw au gratin, fried aubergine or pumpkin fritters.

The seafood is excellent – usually freshly caught, and thoroughly recommended. The island speciality is lobster, with red snapper and other fish as available. An unusual one to try is curried conch.

The tropical climate produces abundant fresh Caribbean vegetables and fruit. Local fruits and vegetables, depending on season, include yams/sweet potato, breadfruit, avocado, green and ripe bananas, papaya, mango, guava and coconut. Renowned for its sweetness is the Antigua black pineapple which is delicious.

The best drinks available are rum based, such as rum punch or planters punch. Most bars will make up drinks that use ice-cold local fruit juices, limes, sugar-cane juice and coconut milk. Try a pineapple daiquiri, made from local pineapples and rum.

Beer is all lager-type, mainly imported from Barbados (Banks) and Jamaica (Red Stripe). Many bars feature discounted drink prices during Happy Hours which can range anywhere from 4 till 8 pm. Two drinks for the price of one is quite normal.

3.9 Nightlife

Evening entertainment is based mainly on what the principal hotels can offer – normally a rotating programme of steel bands, calypso singers, jazz groups, limbo dancing, fashion shows and discos. There are moonlit cruises with dancing, dining and open bar.

Antigua has three casinos: Ramada Renaissance Royal Antiguan Resort & Casino, St James's Club and King's Casino in Heritage Quay. They are American-styled casinos with double-zero roulette, craps, stud poker and a wide selection of slot machines.

Two theatre groups perform at the University. In St John's, local music is played at clubs.

3.10 Quick facts

Total area: 108 sq. miles.

Comparative area: 0.75 times the area of the Isle of Wight; 1.5 times the size of Washington, DC.

Coastline: 95 miles.

Natural resources: negligible; pleasant climate fosters tourism; deeply indented coastline provides many natural harbours.

Land use: arable land 18%; permanent crops 0%; meadows and pastures 7%; forest and woodland 16%; other 59%.

Population: 63,917 growth rate 0.4%.

Life expectancy at birth: 70 years male, 74 years female.

Total fertility rate: 1.7 children born per woman.

Ethnic divisions: almost entirely of black African descent; some of British, Portuguese, Lebanese, and Syrian origin.

Religion: Anglican (predominant), with Methodist, Moravian, Roman Catholic and Baptist denominations represented.

Literacy: 89% (male 90%, female 88%).

Labour force: 30,000; commerce and services 82%, agriculture 11%, industry 7%.

Capital: Saint John's, population 36,000.

Administrative divisions: 6 parishes – Saint George, Saint John, Saint Mary, Saint Paul, Saint Peter, Saint Philip; and 2 dependencies – Barbuda, Redonda.

Independence: 1 November 1981 (from UK).

Government: modelled on the British Parliamentary System, with administration conducted by a Cabinet of Ministers headed by the Prime Minister. Changes of government occur through the democratic process of free elections, held within a period of no longer than five years.

Legal system: based on English common law.

Executive branch: British monarch, governor general, prime minister, deputy prime minister, cabinet.

Legislative branch: two-chamber Parliament with an upper house or Senate and a lower house or House of Assembly.

Judicial branch: Eastern Caribbean Supreme Court.

Political parties: Antigua Labour Party (ALP), United National Democratic Party (UNDP).

Suffrage: universal at age 18.

Economy overview: primarily service oriented, with tourism the most important element in economic performance. During the last decade, real Gross Domestic Product expanded at an annual average rate of about 7%. Tourism's contribution to GDP has risen sharply, and has stimulated growth in other sectors – particularly in construction, communications, and public utilities. Antigua is one of the few areas in the Caribbean experiencing a labour shortage in some sectors of the economy.

Import commodities: petroleum products 48%, manufactures 23%, food and live animals 4%, machinery and transport equipment 17%.

Industries: tourism, construction, light manufacturing - clothing, alcohol, household appliances.

Agriculture: accounts for 4% of GDP; expanding output of cotton, fruits, vegetables, and livestock; other crops - bananas, coconuts, cucumbers, mangoes, sugar-cane; not self-sufficient in food.

Fiscal Year: 1 April-31 March.

3.11 Festivals and Public Holidays

The basic public holidays are:

Jan 1 – New Year's Day
Easter Friday and Monday
1st Monday in May – Labour Day
Whit Monday
2nd Saturday in June – the Queen's official birthday
1st Tuesday in Aug – Carnival Tuesday
1st Monday in Oct – Merchants Holiday, but banks and public offices stay open
Nov 1 – Independence Day
Christmas and Boxing Day.

In addition, the calendar has a good scattering of festivals and sport events. The precise dates change each year, but are most likely to be scheduled in the listed months.

Tennis tournaments are held in January (Men's pro), April (Ladies' pro) – both at the Half Moon Bay Hotel; and in May and October at Curtain Bluff Hotel.

Starting in the last week of April, **Antigua Sailing Week** is a major event in the international yachting calendar, rated among the world's top ten. Held annually since 1967, the regatta Sailing Week attracts around 200 entries from some two dozen countries, to compete in the three major classes - racing, cruiser-racing and cruiser. Contestants gather in the English Harbour area.

Five races are held along the island's western and southern shores. The remaining two days of the week are dedicated to serious party-going, with the final day of Fun and Games in Nelson's Dockyard.

Carnival

The ten days and nights of Carnival, starting in late July and reaching its climax on the first Monday and Tuesday of August, is an explosion of artistic and musical talents. During the build up there's a frenzy of activity as costumes are made in strict secrecy. You can listen to steel bands and calypso singers in the carnival city tents that spring up in the six weeks preceding the grand event. When it happens, Carnival becomes a non-stop party, with street parades and endless music and dance. Holiday visitors are most welcome to join in the fun, jumpin' and jammin' on the streets of St John's.

3.12 Useful addresses

Antiguan High Commission (and Tourist Office), 15 Thayer Street, London W1M 5LD. Tel: 0171 486 7073; Fax: 0171 486 9970.
  Opening hours 9.00-17.30 hrs, Monday to Friday.

Antigua Department of Tourism, 610 Fifth Ave., Suite 311, New York, NY 10020. Tel: 212 541 4117; Fax: 212 757 1607.

Antigua Department of Tourism, 121 S.E. 1st St., Suite 1001, Miami, Florida 33131. Tel: 305 381 6762; Fax: 305 381 7908.

Antigua Department of Tourism, 60 St Clair Ave., Suite 205, Toronto, Ontario MT4 IN5. Tel: 416 961 3085; Fax: 416 961 7218.

Addresses in Antigua: Note that all postal addresses below should end with 'Antigua, West Indies'.

Antigua Department of Tourism, P O Box 363, Thames & Long Streets, St. John's. Open 8-16.30 hrs Mon-Thu; 8-15 hrs Fri. Tel: 462 0029/0480; Fax: 462 2483.

Antigua Hotels Association, Long Street, St. John's. Tel: 462 3702.

British High Commission, 11 Old Parham Way, P O Box 1531 St Johns. Tel: 462 1617/2456/4754/3000.

Emergencies:
Police – 462 0125. **Fire** – 462 0044. **Ambulance** – 462 0251. **Holberton Hospital**, Hospital Road, St. John's: 462 0251.

The International dialling code for Antigua is (010) 1 809, followed by the local 7-digit number.
From North America, start with 1 + 809.
From most other Caribbean islands, and within Antigua itself, just dial the 7-digit number.

Chapter Four

Barbados

4.1 The Barbados Heritage

Sophisticated travellers today are asking "What else besides beaches?" Barbados can offer something more than just the traditional lures of sun, sea and sand. In the competitive world industry of tourism, where every tropical island claims to be an escape to paradise, Barbados is promoting the added value of 'Heritage'.

Known as the Little England of the Caribbean, Barbados was first occupied by English colonists in 1627. They found an uninhabited island. Historians say that the island had been settled 1,500 years earlier by Arawak Indians, who later were overcome by the warlike Caribs. In turn, during the early 16th century, the Caribs were hunted down by the Spaniards who needed slaves for work in Hispaniola – present-day Haiti and the Dominican Republic. Any remaining Caribs soon died from European diseases to which they had no immunity.

When the Portuguese briefly explored the territory in 1536, they called it the Island of the Bearded – Isla de los Barbados – apparently named after the bearded fig trees which grew there. Other linguistic experts claim that the name was inspired by the grizzled banyan trees, whose roots resembled beards.

Both the Portuguese and the Spanish were more interested in making their fortunes in South America; so Barbados was left uninhabited until the English arrived, a century later. The first settlement was established near present-day Holetown on the west coast, followed by a rival settlement three years later at Bridgetown.

The scope for agriculture was good, with reasonably flat land, fertile soil and favourable climate. The first cash crops were tobacco and cotton. Yeoman farmers arrived, to be supplemented later by reluctant Scots, Welsh and Irish who had chosen the wrong side in the English Civil War, and who were exiled to Barbados as bonded servants.

From around 1640, sugar-cane was recognised as the most rewarding product. Only a labour force was lacking. To work the plantations, slaves were imported from Africa. Within a few decades, blacks vastly outnumbered

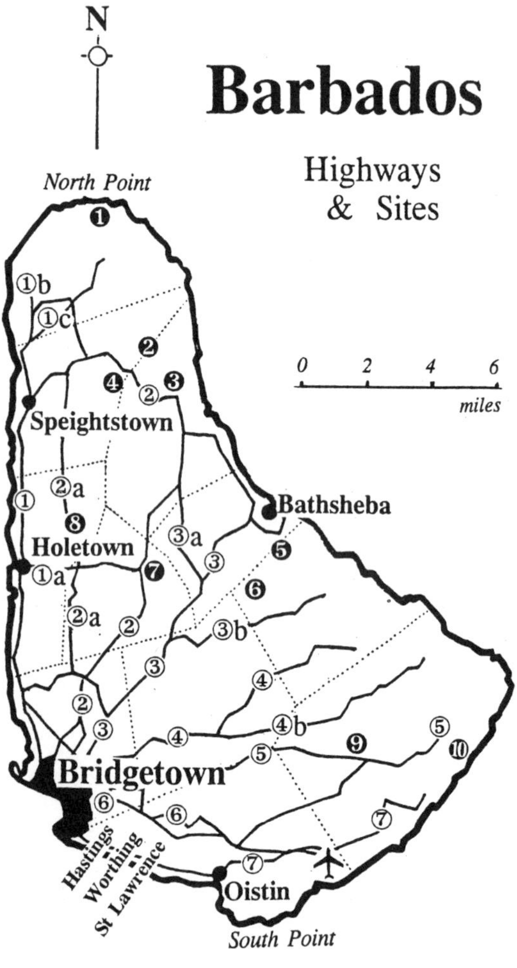

Barbados

Highways & Sites

- ❶ Animal Flower Cave
- ❷ St Nicholas Abbey & Cherry Tree Hill
- ❸ Morgan Lewis Sugar Mill
- ❹ Farley Hill & Barbados Wildlife Reserve
- ❺ Hackleton's Cliff & Andromeda Botanic Gdns.
- ❻ Villa Nova
- ❼ Welchman Hall Gully & Harrison's Cave
- ❽ Portvale Sugar Mill
- ❾ Sunbury House
- ❿ Sam Lord's Castle

①...⑦ Highway nos.

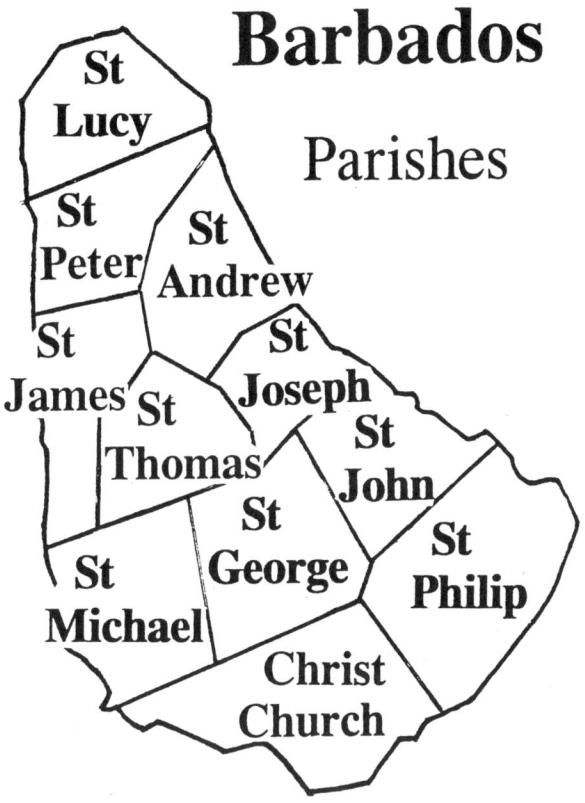

Barbados Parishes

the whites. Import of slaves continued to flourish until the trade was banned by the British parliament in 1807.

Meanwhile, land ownership was vested in a very small group of around twenty families who dominated the island economy. Local parliamentary government was established in 1639, but it was a rubber-stamp operation for whatever the planter elite decided.

However, unlike the wealthy planters in other Carribean islands, who became absentee landlords with a manager left in charge, the 'high whites' of Barbados rarely left their island. They built splendid plantation houses, lived like lords, and set their mark on all the local institutions.

Hence the Heritage: English-style parish churches, horse-racing, the playing of cricket, rugby and polo.

Plantation houses themselves were beautifully equipped with period furniture, and surrounded by landscaped tropical gardens. Despite massive deforestation during the initial rush into sugar, a mixture of imported and homegrown plants created a fine blend of vegetation, from mahogany, palm, casuarina and frangipani to wild roses and carnations.

During the early 20th century, dominance by the small group of planter families continued, until a political rights movement with rioting in 1937 led to foundation of the Barbados Progressive League in 1938. Final independence came on November 30, 1966.

The exceptionally high literacy rate of 98% may contribute to the unusual stability of Barbados. Around 95% of Bajans are coloured. The small white population shares a complicated ancestry ranging from old plantation owners and indentured servants to descendants of the English Civil War political prisoners.

The Bajan (pronounced *Bayj'n*) people today take pride in their national heritage. The calendar contains a wealth of festivals celebrating the island's culture and traditions, past and present. For its small size Barbados is endowed with a rich and elegant architectural legacy, in a setting of great landscape beauty.

Encouraging visitors to discover Barbados' cultural and natural treasures is a high priority for the Barbados Tourism Authority and for the Barbados National Trust. They are committed to making the island's heritage more accessible both to locals and visitors; and also preserving it for future generations.

The National Trust promotes a Heritage Passport which gives admission to the sites and properties under its control. It also sponsors an Open House Programme from January to April, when owners of Stately Homes welcome visitors.

Another popular National Trust venture is a year-round Sunday Hike Programme (and moonlight hikes once a month) exploring areas of historical and natural interest each Sunday of the year. The hikes are popular with Bajans as well as visitors and are an excellent way of meeting local people. Study tours of the island's gardens and architecture are becoming increasingly popular.

Something of the history of Barbados is even reflected in the Bajan dialect, which is a colourful blend of West Country, Welsh and Irish accents, interwoven with the rhythms and linguistic creativity of Africa. If you can't understand what people are saying, "Just be cool and fire a few rums" and all will be well. A more standard form of English is also widely spoken, so visitors have no problems.

Barbados has one of the longest-established tourism infrastructures in the Caribbean. There's a wide range of accommodation from luxury hotels and all-inclusive resorts to rooms in small family guest houses, self-catering cottages and apartments, and top-of-the-range villas. Almost all accommodation gives close access to water-sports on the beaches, and tennis, golf and squash at selected properties.

A plus point is the absence of impersonal, high-rise developments. Buildings are carefully planned to blend into the landscape, enhancing the island's natural beauty.

Despite a high-density population of 250,000, the island only seems crowded on a shopping day in Bridgetown. Bajan people are enormously welcoming and genuinely helpful. The Bajan life-style is laid-back, with a relaxed attitude towards time and punctuality. Visitors soon adjust to the pace. It's no surprise that this 34 km x 22 km island is described by the locals as "just a smile wide".

4.2 Arrival & orientation

Flights from the UK and continental Europe take 7-8 hours for the trans-Atlantic crossing, arriving at Grantley Adams Airport on the southern tip of the island. Located 10 miles from Bridgetown, the airport is handy for most of the island's hotels.

See section 2.2 of this book for general details on passport, Immigration and Customs procedures.

If you need to change cash or travellers cheques, use the exchange facilities before going through Immigration. The services of a Red Cap porter cost 1 US dollar per bag. If you want a porter, it's a good idea to have single Barbados or US dollars handy.

After claiming baggage and clearing Customs, Thomson clients will be met by the local Thomson representative agency Johnson Stables, who arrange the hotel transfers. If you need to contact them, phone 429 5413. For go-it-alone travellers, there are set taxi fares to any island destination. Check the cost first, and clarify whether the cabbie is talking US or Barbadian dollars.

Barbados is a pear-shaped coral limestone island 21 miles long and 14 miles wide (total area 166 sq. miles). The most easterly of the Windward islands, its 3,000 hours a year of tropical sunshine is alleviated by the Northeast Trade Winds which provide a light breeze of average 10 mph.

The West Coast facing the Caribbean is exotic and palm-fringed with gently lapping seas, ideal for snorkelling in the calm waters. Along the South Coast the waves are small to medium, with good breeze for windsurfing.

The East Coast, facing the Atlantic, has great rollers purpose-made for surfers, and the air is fresh and exhilarating. But swimming can be dangerous, and should not be attempted except by very strong swimmers who know the hazards.

From a central spine the land slopes gently to east and west. Highest point of the island is 1,089-ft Mount Hillaby. The west and south-west coasts are the most highly developed for tourism. The capital, Bridgetown, lies at the south-west corner of the island.

All points are easy to reach along the west and south-west coasts; but access is much more tricky around the north and Atlantic-facing coastlines.

Helping modern visitors to get their bearings, settlers in mid-17th century divided the island into 11 parishes with ruler-straight boundaries.

Bridgetown and its suburbs occupy a substantial slice of St Michael parish in the southwest. St James runs northwards along the coast, and includes many of the resort hotels. Christ Church and its southwestern coast is likewise a prime locations for beach resorts.

St Philip, St George and St John occupy the rest of the southern end of Barbados. St Thomas is a central landlocked parish. St Joseph, St Andrew, St Peter and St Lucy fill the northern end of the island.

The easiest way to explore Barbados is parish by parish.

Fanning out from Bridgetown are the island's main highways, numbered clockwise one to seven and reaching to all of the parishes. Running due north along the west coast is Highway 1, which splits off into several fingers – 1A, 1B and 1C. Highway 2 also runs north, with 2A about two miles inland and roughly parallel to Highway 1.

Highway 3 splits into three fingers, to give access to the central part of the east coast. Highways 4 and 4B likewise point you towards the rest of the east coast. Highways 5, 6 and 7 cover the southern end of Barbados.

The ABC Highway acts like an outer ring road around Bridgetown, linking the Airport and the West Coast – a combination of three Highways named alphabetically after three Bajan prime ministers: Tom Adams, Errol Barrow and Gordon Cummins.

Useful free maps are available. It's worth studying the parish and highway layout carefully, before planning trips.

4.3 At your service

Money: The Barbados dollar (Bds$) is tied to the US dollar, two to one. Prices are usually quoted in both currencies at duty-free outlets, and elsewhere on the island. Rates against other currencies fluctuate in line with the US dollar exchange. If sterling is running at US$1.50, then a pound fetches Bds$3. Check local newspapers for the precise rate.

It's best to have cash or travellers cheques in US dollars, but not vital. Small amounts of sterling travellers cheques can be exchanged at hotel and at all banks. Banks are open from 9.00 am – 3.00 pm Mon-Thur and 9.00 am – 1.00 pm and 3.00 pm – 5.00 pm Fri. The most widely accepted credit card is Visa, and American Express is promoted as the 'official' card of Barbados. But all other major credit cards are usually accepted, such as Access/Mastercard and Diners.

Transport: This depends upon whether the priority is price or comfort. The Government-run bus system operates to all corners of the island, using vehicles painted blue with a yellow stripe. Privately-operated minibuses are painted bright yellow with a blue stripe. The standard fare, any distance, is Bds$1.50 a ride (payable on entrance, no tickets). The buses may move rather faster than you would like and be slightly more crowded than you are used to, but it's all part of the holiday thrill. Be prepared for a scrum tackle. Getting a seat is only slightly more subtle.

Otherwise, taxis – marked by the letter 'Z' – are easily available. Remember to check with reception what is the standard printed fare, and agree the price before you climb in. Rates per mile should not exceed Bds$2.50, and daytime waiting time of Bds$7 per hour or Bds$8 per hour after 10 pm. Alternatively there's a flat rate on sightseeing jaunts of Bds$32 per hour. Many of the cabbies have taken a course in guiding.

Automatic and manual cars and mini-mokes can be hired. You will need a local permit (Bds$10 or about £3), available at any police station or through the car rental company on production of your current driving licence. Cost of hire is around £29 per day or £143 upwards per week, plus insurance.

As in Britain, vehicles travel on the left. The principal hazard is the ease of getting lost, especially along winding and unmarked roads amid sugar-cane fields. Take a map! However, the locals are helpful with directions and all roads eventually lead back to Bridgetown.

You'll feel you have been on a journey far longer than the milometer shows, particularly when navigating the island north to south. Driving at night can be especially difficult along roads that are rough and unlit.

Electricity is 110 volts and 50 cycles, using the North American flat 2-pin plug. Check whether any appliances you bring have a dual voltage switch, though some hotels can supply a 240 volt transformer on request. Plug adaptors are available in most department stores, such as Woolworths, Boots and Dixons; and also at the departure airport.

4.4 Places to visit
The architectural and industrial heritage

The great **Plantation Houses** of Barbados had many common design features, developed mainly in response to the climate. They were rarely built more than three storeys high (low profile as protection against occasional hurricanes), with wide verandahs and shuttered jalousie windows. The main building material was the easily-quarried coral limestone which covers most of the island.

Many of the plantation houses recall America's Deep South, and show the influence of classical styles – Palladian, Georgian and Regency – often with a sweeping staircase leading to a front porch with columns and pediment. Although a number of the original great houses have disappeared, some are in care of the National Trust and others can be visited under an Open House programme between January and mid-April.

At the other end of the social scale were the **Chattel Houses**. In response to land laws which enabled freed slaves to own houses but not land, chattel houses were made of wood for mobility and placed on a sill of stone blocks. Despite their small size, they often simulated the shuttered windows and verandahs of the great houses. Many chattel houses still remain around the island, adding charm to the landscape. Decorated in vivid colours, they make a favourite photo subject.

The Barbados National Trust also maintains several examples of the island's industrial heritage, mostly connected with the sugar industry.

Bridgetown and St Michael's parish – the highlights

The capital itself, population 100,000, was founded 1628 by settlers sponsored by the Earl of Carlisle. The town was named after an Indian-built bridge across the narrow sea inlet which made such an ideal harbour.

Trafalgar Square – The city's central hub, honouring Lord Nelson who frightened off the French in 1805, but who then lost his life at Trafalgar later in the year. His statue was erected by grateful planters in 1813 – thirty years before London paid similar tribute. The dolphin fountain commemorates the arrival of piped water into Bridgetown in 1861.

The Careenage is the lively natural harbour where schooners were careened and refitted. Today the jetties are lined with luxury yachts and small fishing boats, while larger vessels dock at the Deep Water Harbour further west. A former warehouse on the southern bank is now the Waterfront Cafe, offering a superb view.

Chamberlain Bridge – Crosses from Trafalgar Square to Independence Square, and separates the Careenage from the Inner Basin. It was named after Joseph Chamberlain, the British Colonial Secretary who saved the island sugar trade by his turn-of-the-century policies of colonial preference.

Independence Square is a popular venue for political meetings.

The Public Buildings – Facing Trafalgar Square, the third oldest Parliamentary institution of the English-speaking world, established in 1639. The present 19th-century buildings accommodate both the Senate and the House of Assembly, which for 30 years in the 17th century met in taverns.

The Bridgetown Synagogue – From 1654 a community of Sephardic Jews worshipped here, but mostly they migrated elsewhere in mid-19th century, and the structure fell into decay. In recent times the building has been beautifully restored and is again used for prayer. Claimed as the oldest synagogue in the Western hemisphere, it is open to visitors 9-16 hrs, Mon-Fri.

Broad Street – The city's principal commercial street, the centre for financial institutions and high-grade shopping.

Cheapside Market – Beyond Broad Street and near St Mary's church, the fruit and vegetable market is busiest on Saturdays. South of the Cheapside Market in the Temple Yard district is the main Rastafarian enclave, with Africa-inspired crafts on sale in a colourful splash of red, green and gold.

Pelican Village – A 3-acre arts and crafts complex along Princess Alice Highway near Deep Water Harbour. Visitors can watch craftsmen at work, and can buy the products. Serious art is displayed at the Barbados Arts Council Gallery. The Bajan sculptor Karl Broodhagen and the potter Courtney Devonish have studios here.

St. Michael's Cathedral – Built of coral rock in 1789 after the original wooden church of 1665 was destroyed by a hurricane. Soaring above the cathedral's skyline is the 11-storey **Central Bank** – highest building in Barbados – which also houses the **Frank Collymore Hall**, a well-equipped 500-seat concert hall.

Fairchild Market – Liveliest on Saturday mornings. The main Bus Terminal is close by.

Queen's Park – The former residence of the military commander of the West Indies, but abandoned in 1906. A public park, its main attraction is a 1,000-year-old baobab tree, over 60 feet in circumference. The house itself has been converted into a theatre and restaurant.

Along Bay Street and around Carlisle Bay, Highway 7 leads to the **Garrison Historic Area**, where British troops were stationed from 1694-1906. Varied forts and buildings have been restored. In the **National Cannon Collection**, the guns date mainly from the 17th century, and comprise one of the world's largest collections of cannon from that period. The huge parade ground, called the Savannah, is today's setting for the **Garrison Savannah Racetrack**.

The former Garrison prison has been converted to happier use as **The Barbados Museum**, displaying a broad collection of artifacts from old-time Barbados. Open 9-18 hrs Mon-Sat. Entry Bds$7. The courtyard is used for evening performances of "1627 and all that", when the museum rooms can be viewed at no extra charge.

Outwards from central Bridgetown, past Queens Park, leads to **Government House**. This was formerly a Quaker-owned residence, bought in 1736 as permanent quarters for the Governor of Barbados. The architecture is in the typical style of a sugar planter's mansion.

Ilaro Court dates from 1919, and was built by the wife of a former Governor. The coral stone property is set in an immaculate landscape amid splendid mahogany trees. Since 1976 Ilaro Court has been the Prime Minister's official residence.

If you drive further out on Highway 5, watch for **The Emancipation Statue – 'Bussa'** at the crossroads with Errol Barrow Highway. It commemorates the freeing of slaves in 1834. Bussa was the leader of a slave revolt in 1816. The sculptor was Karl Broodhagen, whose studio is located at Pelican Village.

Tyrol Cot, on Highway 2. Renovated by the National Trust, Tyrol Cot was the home from 1929 of Barbados' first Prime Minister, Sir Grantley Adams, who founded the Barbados Labour Party. Built in 1854, Tyrol Cot combined Palladian influences with tropical style, particularly with its arched and shuttered windows. The intention is to feature chattel houses and a craft village within the grounds.

University of the West Indies – The campus overlooks Bridgetown on Cave Hill between Highway 1 and Cummings Highway. Opened in 1963, faculties include Law, Education and Natural Sciences. Other faculties of the University are located in Jamaica and Trinidad and Tobago.

Quite close, to the north, is **Lazaretto Gardens** – named after a former leper house – with a splendid waterfall in a landscaped setting. The National Archives are located here.

Christ Church Parish

Here is the coast that pioneered the Barbados tourist industry, based on a necklace of sandy beaches and rolling surf. Highway 7 serves the coastal belt from Hastings to the fishing village of Oistin, giving easy access to the ribbon development of hotels, apartments and guesthouses. Nightlife is centred especially along **St Lawrence Gap** at Worthing.

For a change of scenery, birdlovers enjoy the **Graeme Hall Swamp** – the island's largest area of inland water, with resident and migrant birds amid an 80-acre sanctuary of sedge and mangroves: a particularly favourable habitat for white egrets and yellow warblers.

Oistins is the island's main fishing port, served by a modern terminal. At sunset, watching the laid-back fishermen helming in with their feet must be one of the island's most relaxing sights. Above the town is **Christ Church Parish Church**, best known for the Great Coffin Mystery which baffled investigators in the 1810s. How did lead coffins jump around in a sealed vault?

At the furthest tip of the island is **South Point Lighthouse**, prefabricated in cast iron for display at London's Great Exhibition of 1851, and then erected here in 1852.

St George Parish

Highways 3 and 4 are the main access routes into this landlocked parish dedicated to sugarcane galore.

Francia Plantation House near Gun Hill is an elegant 20th-century family home built for the original French owner of this working plantation growing cane, yams, eddoes and sweet potatoes. Furnishings are mainly 19th-century, but the walls are decorated with antique maps including a West Indies' map printed in 1522. The terraced gardens are a delight. Open Mon-Fri 10-16 hrs. Entry Bds$6.

Gun Hill Signal Station is an 1818 hilltop tower which offers a sweeping view of the southern end of the island. Open daily 9-17 hrs. Entry Bds$5.

Drax Hall is a Jacobean-style mansion built in mid-16th century by the original Sir James Drax who pioneered the cultivation and manufacture of sugar on his 858-acre estate. Among the oldest of the island's plantation houses, Drax Hall is unique in still being owned by the same family.

St Thomas Parish

North of St George Parish is St Thomas, which likewise is landlocked. Highways 1A, 2 and 2A give access.

Bagatelle Great House – Now a well-known gourmet restaurant, Bagatelle House is one of the finest surviving examples of the Barbadian style of architecture. Built around the 1650's it has extremely thick walls and is Palladian influenced, with a classic double staircase leading to a front porch with columns and pediment. Location is off Highway 2A.

Harrison's Cave – on Highway 2, this is the only limestone cave system of its kind open to the public in the Caribbean. The beauty of the stalactites and stalagmites is enhanced by lighting effects. Visitors travel for a mile through the caverns, aboard a special tram and trailer, to a 40-ft waterfall and lake at the lowest point of the complex. Open daily 9-16 hrs, with 45-minute tours every hour. Entry Bds$15.

Welchman Hall Gully – a close neighbour of Harrison's Cave, and owned by the National Trust. Created by the collapse of a cave system, the half-mile gully is filled with hundreds of exotic trees and plants, including rare species of clove and nutmeg. It gives some idea of the original jungle that covered Barbados when the first settlers arrived in 1627. Open daily 9-17 hrs. Entry Bds$5.

St James Parish

Occupying the central stretch of the sandy-beach 'platinum coast', St James is a wealthy paradise of luxury hotels and extremely expensive villas. Highway 1 hugs the coast.

Holetown – Site of the first English settlement, it was named out of sailors' nostalgia for Limehouse Hole on the River Thames. Very little remains of the original James Fort, but the past is celebrated annually in the Holetown Festival of mid February.

St James Parish Church in Holetown was built 1785 to replace its predecessor, wrecked by a hurricane.

Folkestone Underwater Park & Museum – Just north of Holetown, the small museum features an aquarium and other items of marine interest. Open daily 10-17 hrs. Entry Bds$1. From Folkestone beach there is access for snorkellers and scuba divers to reach an underwater trail along the protected inshore reef. An artificial reef has been created by the sinking of a ship named *Stavronikita*. The underwater park can also be viewed from glass-bottomed boats.

Portvale Sugar Factory on Highway 2 is a modernised plant producing 1,500 tons of sugar every week of the grinding season, February to May. During the season, visits can be arranged, usually on Wednesdays, by phoning 432 6748. Adjoining the factory is the **Sir Frank**

Hutson Sugar Machinery Museum which houses a unique collection of machinery from the industry's past.

St Peter Parish

North of St. James Parish, St Peter is served by Highways 1 and 1C, 2 and 2A. It reaches across the island from the west coast to a narrow strip of east coast.

Speightstown is the island's 2nd-largest town, named after a Bristol merchant called Speight. Because of a continued close connection with Bristol for export of sugar, it was locally known as 'Little Bristol'. In the centre, protected from through traffic, the narrow streets of two-storey wooden buildings show little change from the past hundred years.

Farley Hill National Park – This elegant Georgian/Regency style mansion is now a picturesque ruin. Following its glory days in the second half of the 19th century, the house fell into neglect. It enjoyed a brief burst of fame as a location for the film "Island in the Sun" but was destroyed by fire in the 1960's. The site was bought by the Government and opened as a National Park in 1966.

Open daily 7-18 hrs. Entry cars Bds$3.

Barbados Wildlife Reserve – Across the highway from Farley Hill Park, this small sanctuary allows you to view Barbados Green Monkeys, deer, parrots, tortoise and alligators at close quarters, while you take a leisurely stroll through four acres of lush mahogany woodland. Scattered around are varied artifacts of old-time sugar factories.

The reserve is operated by the Barbados Primate Research Project Centre. Open daily 10-17 hrs. Entry Bds$10.

St Nicholas Abbey – Built around 1650-60, this Jacobean mansion is one of only three buildings of its type in the New World. The three-storied facade has the curving gables often seen on English manors of that time. The present owner has worked with the National Trust to restore and furnish the house and its surroundings to their old splendour.

Open Mon-Fri 10-15 hrs. Entry Bds$5.

St Lucy Parish

Here is the rugged Atlantic coastline of the northern end of Barbados, with access along fingers of Highway 1, and also along Charles Duncan O'Neale Highway, which is an extension of Highway 2.

Mount Gay Distillery – Established in 1663, this distillery claims to be the oldest in Barbados. The present 19th-century plant produces half a million gallons of rum annually, and is open to visitors between 8 and 16 hrs. But there are also more conveniently located tours at the ageing and blending facility on Spring Garden Highway, just outside Bridgetown. Open Mon-Fri 9-17 hrs; Sat 10-13 hrs. Entry Bds$8, tasting included. Tel: 425 8757.

Animal Flower Cave – At North Point, just before you fall off the end of the island. You can watch the Atlantic crashing against the coral cliffs, or venture into the sea caves under the cliffs, if accessible. The cave gets its name from the tiny sea anemones that grow in its pools. Open daily 9-17 hrs. Entry Bds$3.

St Andrew Parish

For early Scottish settlers, the rolling hills and grazing sheep were a reminder of their homeland. Hence, much of this parish was named the Scotland District. With small population, the scenery has not changed much. Highway 2 is the principal access.

Good viewpoints are **Mount Hillaby** (the island's highest point at 1,115 ft), **Cherry Tree Hill** (with a fine avenue of mahogany trees) and **Chalky Mount** (where local potters still use old-time wheels).

Morgan Lewis Sugar Mill, just south of Cherry Tree Hill, processed sugarcane until the arrival of powered machinery. It is the largest and only complete surviving sugar windmill in the Caribbean. Its Dutch design is attributed to the Dutch Jews who introduced sugar cultivation and technology from Brazil in the 17th century.

Open Mon-Fri 9-17 hrs. Entry Bds$2.

St Joseph Parish

A continuation of the Scotland District into this smallest parish of Barbados offers many fine viewpoints along the breezy coastline. The **East Coast Road** – linking the coastal ends of Highways 3 and 3A – was opened by Queen Elizabeth in 1966. It follows the track of an old railway line.

Hackleton's Cliff offers a dramatic coastal view, from 1,000 feet above. A path leads to **Joe's River Tropical Rain Forest**, where nature trails open up 85 forested acres which include the Bearded Fig Trees that reputedly led Portuguese navigators to name the land as Isla de los Barbados.

Bathsheba – A fishing village where the locals 'cool out' on the wild and rugged Atlantic coast. Admire the magnificent views and the sheer natural beauty, but be cautious about swimming as the currents are dangerous. The "Soup Bowl" is the annual venue for champion surfing events.

Andromeda Botanic Gardens near Bathsheba is National Trust property. This gardener's delight was created in 1954 by Mrs Iris Bannochie whose family had owned the land for 200 years. Six acres of exotic plants and flowers include orchids, heliconias, palms and cacti set on a cliff overlooking the coast. Open daily 8 a.m. till sunset. Entry Bds$8.

Flower Forest of Barbados, reached via Highway 2 or 3A, is another gardener's delight – a landscaped area of tropical flowers and trees with spectacular views over the island. Monkeys can often be seen in the early morning or at dusk.
  Open daily 9-17 hrs. Entry Bds$10.

St John Parish

Hackleton's cliff is shared with St Joseph parish – see above -and the southern end is marked by St John Parish Church, just off Highway 3B.

Villa Nova – Rebuilt of coral stone after an 1831 hurricane and set in wooded grounds, Villa Nova has many of the typical features of a Barbadian great house – wide verandahs, "jalousie" shutters and a parapet to protect against hurricanes. Once owned by Sir Anthony Eden, it has been restored by its current owners and is open to the public Mon-Fri 10-16 hrs. Entry Bds$5.

Codrington College can be approached via Highway 4. The site was originally the 17th-century plantation home of sugar planter Christopher Codrington who left the property to the Society for the Propagation of the Gospel in Foreign Parts. The College began operation in 1745, and is now part of the University of the West Indies. The clifftop campus overlooks **Consett Bay**, where fishermen land their catch most afternoons.

St Philip Parish

Highways 4B, 5, 6 and 7 give access to the island's largest parish which occupies the eastern corner of Barbados, facing the Atlantic.

Sunbury Plantation House goes back to the 1660's when sugar established great family fortunes. This early 18th-century Plantation House is furnished in Victorian style with traditional mahogany and other antiques. The museum section displays costumes, elegant horse carriages, carts, implements and tools used on a West Indian plantation during 18th and 19th centuries.
  Access along Highway 5. Open daily 10-16.30 hrs. Entry Bds$8. On some evenings the staff serve a candle-lit Bajan dinner. Reservations: 423 6270.

Oughterson National Wildlife Park on Highway 4B is a 22-acre wildlife breeding centre with an educational purpose. Admission to Oughterson House is included in the entry fee of Bds$8. Open Mon-Sat 9-17 hrs; Sun 10.15-17.00 hrs.

Sam Lord's Castle is now a luxury-grade Marriott Hotel, but the main structure of the original Regency mansion can be visited. Sam Lord was a planter with a dubious reputation as a ship wrecker. He lavished his money on magnificent decoration and furnishing of his Castle. Entry Bds$5.

4.5 Take a trip

Tear yourself away from the beaches, and explore the rich island history and culture. Your tour rep can answer questions, give information, book excursions or organise a hire car or mini-moke.

Taxis make a comfortable alternative to low-cost buses, at reasonable cost if shared with your fellow hotel guests. Guided tours, with all the details ready organised, give door-to-door service from all the main hotels.

An all-day **Island Tour** costing about £35 including lunch is a good way to get an overall picture of the variety of Barbados' scenery. Enjoy the views from Farley Hill on the east coast, hear the yarns about Sam Lord's Castle and admire the sweeping fields of sugar cane.

In more leisured style, a series of half-day trips costing around £20 can focus in detail on selected aspects of the island. Typical is the **Harrison's Cave and Flower Forest** tour, which focusses on the subterranean and floral highlights. Other options can look more closely at the great Plantation Houses.

Rum tours feature a visit to the West India Rum Refinery, the home of world-renowned Cockspur Rum. A lavish Bajan buffet lunch is served in the typical atmosphere of a rum shop complete with a steel band. Price is around Bds$55.

Sunday Hike Programme – every Sunday the Barbados National Trust runs morning and afternoon hikes (and moonlight hikes once a month) exploring areas of historical and natural interest . Experienced guides lead the hikes which are graded into "fast", "medium" and "stop and stare". The excursions are popular with Bajans as well as visitors. They are an excellent way of meeting local people, while learning more about the geography and culture of Barbados.

Boat trips – There are several possibilities of enjoyable cruises along the coast of Barbados or to other islands. Typical is the **Jolly Roger Cruise.** Your holiday will go with a swing as you watch your spouse walk the plank into the ocean. A lunch-time barbecue, rum punch galore (and other liquids) and entertainment are included on this half-day trip costing approx Bds$105 (£35).

For seeing marine life in depth, take a one-hour cruise aboard the **Atlantis submarine** - a 50-ft Canadian-built boat designed to operate down to 150 feet. The vessel has eight large portholes each side, with seating for two people at each porthole. In the crystal-clear water you can view the shoals of tropical fish in their natural habitat among the sponge and coral formations. Eyeball to eyeball, marine life cruises past the portholes, just accepting the submarine as another big fish. Based at The Careenage, Bridgetown, the boat takes 28 passengers with a guide to comment on the passing scene. On night trips, powerful spotlights are used.

4.6 All the sports

During your stay you can enjoy some of the best sports facilities in the Caribbean, both on land and water. All the main hotels are geared especially to watersports. At the all-inclusive resorts, use of equipment is mostly available at no extra charge. Otherwise, here's a rough indication of prices:

Waterskiing – Fairly easy once you get on your feet! Approx Bds$35 (£12) for 15 mins.

Snorkelling – See the most beautiful marine life in the clear blue waters, best along the west coast. Rent of equipment costs about Bds$20 (£7) an hour.

Scuba Diving – After a few days of training, the amazing world of coral reefs and sunken wrecks will open up. Reckon Bds$90 per dive with equipment (£30). Decompression chamber now in operation. A reminder: it is forbidden to disturb the reef by removing pieces of coral. Don't stand on the reef, break it or touch it. Spearguns are banned.

Windsurfing – Especially good along the southern coastline, with steady breezes. It's worth making a special trip to Silver Sands at South Point. Approx Bds$30 (£10) per hour.

Parasailing – Sightseeing with a difference high above the island. Around Bds$80 (£27) for 10 mins.

In January, watersports enthusiasts can watch or take part in windsurfing and yachting at the Barbados International Windsurfing Classics which are held each year.

Land-based sports

Golf – There are three golf courses. At Sandy Lane is the island's only 18-hole (soon to be 27-hole) championship golf course. At Rockley Resort (Club Barbados) and at the Heywoods Resort are 9-hole courses. The Sandy Lane

Open takes place over three days in November.

Tennis – All major hotels have good courts, some illuminated for evening play before the cocktails get going. Some public courts are government run, and most can be used by visitors.

Squash – Courts are available at three major centres, all air-conditioned.

Spectator sports

The Barbados Turf Club runs 20 race meetings a year on alternate Saturdays from January to April, and August to November. The biggest racing event is the Cockspur Gold Cup Race in March. This major Caribbean event has become so popular that the week before is now celebrated as "Gold Cup Week" with many colourful pageants.

Kensington Oval is the venue for major cricket games, with cricket at all levels taking place everywhere on the island. Beware those Barbadian fast bowlers! July and August are the months for Sir Garfield Sobers International Schools' Cricket Tournament, designed to encourage young cricketers from all over the world.

In October, the new Barbados Aquatic Centre hosts the **International Masters Meet** for local, regional and international swimmers. **International Surfing Championships** are held in November.

4.7 Shopping

Shops are generally open 8-16 hrs Monday-Friday and 8-12 hrs on Saturdays. Post Offices open 8-12 and 13-15 hrs Monday-Friday.

The fullest possible range of shopping is available in Bridgetown, especially along Broad Street, starting from Trafalgar Square. A wide variety of imported luxury items - jewelry, perfume, photographic and electronic gear – can be bought duty free. Produce your flight ticket and passport and make your purchases at least 24 hours before you leave the island. Some tax-free goods can be taken away at the time of sale. Other purchases (notably liquor and tobacco) have to be delivered to the airport terminal for collection on departure. Caution: don't be dazzled by the 'duty-free' publicity. Be sure you know the price back home, and remember there's Customs to face for any major purchase.

At the airport, your goodies can be reclaimed from a special and clearly marked desk, on production of the relevant receipts. There are also several duty-free shops in the departure lounge.

Similar shopping facilities are located at other centres, including Holetown, Speightstown, Oistins, Hastings and Worthing. Also worth exploring are Petticoat Lane at Bridgetown Wharf; and high fashion boutiques at Sandy Lane, Glitter Bay and Royal Pavilion. "Simon" at Paynes Bay, St James, offers exotic beach and evening clothes.

Handicrafts are sold at beach vendors' stalls, at any of the "Best of Barbados" shop locations, or at Pelican Village (a 3-acre complex along Princess Alice Highway on the outskirts of Bridgetown near Deep Water Harbour). Best buys include local paintings (as pictures or on place mats, coasters, etc), T-shirts and beach-wraps, batik, leather goods, pottery, local wood and wicker craft, hats and bowls styled from woven palm leaves.

Coral is on sale as giftware or coral jewellery. Refuse to buy! Remember that coral forms an intricate part of marine life. To purchase it only encourages those who plunder the seabeds. You may also have problems with Customs on returning home, as import of coral is banned by all countries that respect the environment.

Among the **Art Galleries**, check the following for what's on show:
- Bertalan Sculpture Studios, Marine Gardens, Christchurch. Tel: 427 0414.
- Devonish Gallery, Pelican Village, St. Michael.
- Stella St John Studios, Enterprise Road, Christchurch.
- Talma Mill Art Gallery, Enterprise Road, Christchurch. Tel: 428 9383.
- Queen's Park Gallery is the island's largest gallery, and is run by the National Cultural Foundation. Tel: 427 2345.
- Barbados Arts Council Gallery, Pelican Village. Tel: 426 4385.

4.8 Eating out

Bajan food is natural and good. Sample some flying fish Bajan-style with cou-cou (maize meal), or fried plantain (not a weed, but a vegetable banana), sweet potatoes, breadfruit (substitute for potato), peas 'n' rice (rice and split peas boiled and spiced together) and Creole dishes for those who like it hot.

The cuisine, like Bajan history, is a melting pot. To sample a typical local dinner in Barbados is to taste and smell the influences – African, European and Asian – that have made Barbados what it is today.

The "national dish" of cou-cou and salt fish is a good illustration of how and why the Bajan style of cooking has developed. Originally adopted as a cheap way to feed plantation workers, this cornmeal and okra pudding (African inspired but similar to "grits" and polenta) is bland but nourishing. It was served with cheap imported salt fish and cooked with herbs and spices to give it flavour. Cou-cou and salt fish has retained its place in the affections of Bajans, even though salt fish is now as expensive as meat and poultry.

Barbados has abundant supplies of fresh fish and seafood. The ubiquitous flying fish and its traditional seasoning of finely chopped onion, parsley, black and red peppers, salt, garlic and lime, are popular everywhere from the humblest beach bar to the grandest restaurant. Always a winner is a flying fish sandwich – especially good with a rum punch, after a beach stroll or a swim.

There are many other fish available at various times of the year: red snapper, grouper, marlin, kingfish, swordfish and crustaceans such as lobster, shrimps and crab. Callaloo is a soup of crabmeat with okra and a vegetable like spinach.

Meat is less common. Many country families just keep a pig and some free-range chickens. It is said that the only part of the pig Bajans are unable to convert into food is the hair. Trotters and tails often flavour vegetable dishes, while the head and belly are steeped overnight in lime juice with cucumber, onions and peppers to make the dish called Souse. Other bits and pieces are made into the spicy sausage known as Pudding.

Bajans are proud of their cuisine. Groaning buffets with a vast array of traditional dishes make up Sunday meals both in private homes and in restaurants and hotels.

The local cuisine is celebrated publicly in an annual exhibition each autumn, Bajan Table, sponsored by the Hotels Association; and in the culinary arts section of the National Independence Festival of the Creative Arts each November.

Apart from all these localized taste experiences, Barbados boasts a full range of sophisticated restaurants which cater for an international clientele. All the main hotels feature the great culinary traditions of Europe or the Orient.

The Barbados Tourism Authority operates a grading system for restaurants: One knife and fork indicates a good restaurant where simplicity is the keynote; Two knives and forks for restaurants with a higher standard of comfort and facilities; Three knives and forks for exceptionally well appointed restaurants with a separate lounge. A rosette is awarded to establishments with above average cuisine and service within the classification.

Most hotels and restaurants have a good selection of imported wines, but visitors should sample the rum-based cocktails before or after dinner, or while "cooling' out and limin' around". Many bars feature a Happy Hour until around 7 pm, giving visitors the chance of exploring the range.

Among the more unusual potions is Mauby, a tart but refreshing drink, made by boiling the bark of the mauby tree with vanilla essence and spices. Another local invention is Falernum, which incorporates ground almonds, clove powder, brown sugar, ginger, and lime juice. Mixed with rum, it's called 'corn 'n oil'. A Barbados bombshell is a powerful mixture of Pernod, rum, crushed limes and grenadine syrup.

The most popular beers are locally-brewed Banks and Jubilee Ale, while Red Stripe is imported from Jamaica.

Finally, here's a short list of well-known restaurants. Ask your tour rep for other recommendations, closer to wherever you are staying. The full list of international-grade restaurants runs to over a hundred.

Reids – Opposite Coconut Creek, St James. Excellent service and food. Romantic, intimate dining with pretty gardens and fountains. From Bds$99 (£33) including wine.

Carambola – Pretty ocean-side setting just south of Coconut Creek. Open-air dining, romantic and good food. From Bds$89 – 99 (around £30) with wine.

Fishermans Wharf – Overlooking the Careenage and its yachts. Pretty, breezy location and excellent food and service. From Bds$79 (£26) with wine.

Da Luciano's – Elegant Italian restaurant, just south of Bridgetown. The menu includes pasta as well as fish and meat dishes. Beautifully decorated intimate old house. Pricey - from Bds$60-110 (up to £38) with wine.

4.9 Nightlife

Virtually all the big hotels offer a weekly programme of cabarets, discos, theme nights and folklore shows with steel bands, calypso singers, fire eaters and limbo dancers. Many visitors who aren't on a full-board arrangement go hotel-hopping each evening. You are welcome to drop in for a drink at the bar without entrance charge in most hotels. But it's advisable to book ahead for popular restaurants which are full every night. At discos, there's an admission charge for non-residents, but the reggae and calypso are unforgettable.

Among the most popular nightspots are **The Warehouse** overlooking the careenage waterfront in Bridgetown, and **After Dark** at St Lawrence Gap, Christ Church. A favourite open-air beachfront disco is **Harbour Lights** on Bay Street, Bridgetown, with live music after 22 hrs. The entertainment programme and price structure changes nightly. The lights go out around 4.30 a.m.

If you survive until then and feel peckish, why not try some of **Enid & Livy's** incomparable chicken in Baxter Road, where numerous little eating-places do lively trade from 11 p.m. onwards? You will find your way home more easily once the sun has come up!

In more formal style are excellent dinner shows wrapped around an evening of dancing, calypso singing, flamboyant costumes and good local buffet. These can be booked through your hotel or tour rep. Some top choices are:

Tropical Spectacular and **Barbados by Night** – Popular dinner shows featured by The Plantation restaurant at St Lawrence, Christ Church. Excellent buffet, open bar and magnificent show with dazzling costumes. Dinner starts at 18.30 hrs, the show at 20 hrs. After the show, give your own feet some exercise on the dance floor. Cost is Bds$90 (£30), transport to and from your hotel included. Or you can take the show only for Bds$40.

"1627 and all that" – Sunday and Thursday evenings at Barbados Museum on the Garrison Savannah. It's a cultural romp through history with a Bajan-style dinner during the two-part folklore show, which includes a live steel band. Cost: Bds$85 all-in.

Another night-time possibility is to embark aboard the **Bajan Queen** – a Mississippi style of river boat which features music, dancing, buffet dinner and open bar during a cruise along the west coast, starting with the splendour of a Caribbean sunset.

4.10 Quick facts

Total area: 166 sq. miles.

Comparative area: slightly larger than the Isle of Wight; 2.5 times the size of Washington, DC.

Coastline: 60 miles.

Natural resources: crude oil, fishing, natural gas.

Land use: arable land 77%; permanent crops 0%; meadows and pastures 9%; forest and woodland 0%; other 14%.

Population: 255,000, growth rate 0.1%.

Life expectancy at birth: 70 years male, 76 years female.

Total fertility rate: 1.8 children born per woman.

Ethnic divisions: African 80%, mixed 16%, European 4%.

Religion: Protestant 67% (Anglican 40%, Pentecostal 8%, Methodist 7%, other 12%), Roman Catholic 4%; none 17%, unknown 3%, other 9%. Over 100 religious groups are represented in Barbados.

Literacy: 99%.

Labour force: 112,300; services and government 37%; commerce 22%; manufacturing and construction 22%;

transportation, storage, communications, and financial institutions 9%; agriculture 8%; utilities 2%.

Capital: Bridgetown, population 100,000 including suburbs.

Administrative divisions: 11 parishes; Christ Church, Saint Andrew, Saint George, Saint James, Saint John, Saint Joseph, Saint Lucy, Saint Michael, Saint Peter, Saint Philip, Saint Thomas; and the city of Bridgetown.

Independence: 30 November 1966 (from UK).

Government: Barbados is an independent country within the British Commonwealth with a parliamentary system of government. **Legal system**: based on English common law.

Executive branch: British monarch, governor general, prime minister, deputy prime minister, cabinet.

Legislative branch: two-chamber Parliament with an upper house or Senate and a lower house or House of Assembly.

Judicial branch: Supreme Court of Judicature.

Political parties: Democratic Labour Party (DLP); Barbados Labour Party (BLP); National Democratic Party (NDP).

Suffrage: universal at age 18.

Economy overview: A per capita income of US $6,500 gives Barbados one of the highest living standards of the eastern Caribbean. Historically, the economy was based on sugar and rum. More recently Barbados has diversified into manufacturing and tourism. The tourist industry has become a major employer and a prime source of foreign earnings. High unemployment remains serious. **Export commodities**: sugar and molasses, electrical components, clothing, rum, machinery and transport equipment.

Industries: tourism, sugar, light manufacturing, component assembly for export.

Agriculture: accounts for 10% of GDP; major cash crop is sugarcane; other crops – vegetables and cotton; not self-sufficient in food.

Fiscal Year: 1 April-31 March.

4.11 Festivals & holidays

The basic public holidays are:

Jan 1 – New Year's Day
3rd Monday in Jan – Errol Barrow Day
Easter Friday and Monday
May 1 – May Day
Whit Monday
1st Monday in Aug – Kadooment Day
1st Monday in Oct – United Nations Day
Nov 30 – Independence Day
Christmas and Boxing Day

In addition, the calendar is filled with festivals that celebrate the island, past and present. In recent years, sport and music festivals have also become popular with participants from around the world competing or participating. Here's a month-by-month selection of events. The precise dates change each year, but will most likely occur in the listed months. Check dates and programmes with the Barbados Tourism Authority – see addresses in next section, 4.12.

January – The well-established three-day **Regatta**, sponsored by Mount Gay Rum and formerly held during the Christmas period, is now moved to the end of January, to coincide with arrival of yachts racing trans-ocean in the **Mount Gay Atlantic Barbados Challenge**.

Between January and mid-April, an **Open House Programme** is organised by the Barbados National Trust. Every Wednesday afternoon from 14.30-17.30 hrs, houses of historical or architectural interest are opened to visitors. Local horticultural enthusiasts also open their gardens to the public every Sunday in January, leading to the Annual Flower Show in February.

February – Horse racing at Garrison Savannah; Cricket's Red Stripe Competition; amateur boxing; Horticultural Society's annual flower show.

A major event is the week-long **Holetown Festival**, to commemorate the landing of the first settlers in February 1627. Traditional celebrations include street fairs, arts and crafts, and music.

March – Horses from other Caribbean islands participate in the prestigious 9-furlong **Cockspur Gold Cup Race** at Garrison Savannah racecourse.

Sandy Lane Open Golf Championship is held. An **Easter Festival** is planned to spread over the two weeks before Good Friday, with a varied programme of polo, opera and Shakespeare.

April – During the Easter holiday, the **Oistins Fish Festival** celebrates the life and contribution which this fishing town has made to the island's development.

Offering a strong flavour of the sea, the programme focusses on fishing and boat-related activities, with craft shows, food stalls and dancing. Highlights include a Fish Boning Competition between fishermen and fish vendors, crab racing and many bands and singers.

Another traditional Easter event is an **Easter Bonnet Parade** in Bridgetown.

May – Something different: **Gospelfest** – towards the end of the month, a gospel music festival which was successfully launched in 1993.

July/August – The highlight of the cultural calendar, the **Crop-Over Festival** merges the old plantation traditions that marked the end of the sugar-cane harvest, with the more modern style of Carnival. Starting with the ceremonial Delivery of the Last Canes, the festival builds to the grand finale of **Kadooment** on the first Monday in August, when Bridgetown is surrendered to street fairs, calypso music, dance and a costumed band parade.

November – Running right through the month, the **National Independence Festival of Creative Arts (NIFCA)** has developed as a forum for Bajans to express their creative talents in the arts. The festival culminates on Independence Day, November 30, with a gala presentation featuring all the finalists.

December – In the first weekend, the **Run Barbados Road Race** comprises a 10K and a Marathon, and attracts international runners.

4.12 Useful addresses

Barbados High Commission, 1 Great Russell Street, London WC1B 3NH. Tel (0171) 631 4975.

Barbados Tourism Authority, 263 Tottenham Court Road, London W1P 9AA. Tel (0171) 636 9448.
Opening hours: 9.30-17.30 hrs Monday to Friday.

Barbados Tourism Authority, 800 2nd Ave., New York, NY 10017. Tel: 212 986 6516; Toll free: 800 221 9831; Fax: 212 573 9850.

Barbados Tourism Authority, 3440 Wiltshire Blvd., Suite 1215, Los Angeles, Calif 90010. Tel: 213 380 2198; Toll free: 800 221 9831; Fax: 213 384 2763.

Barbados Tourism Authority, 5160 Yonge St., Suite 1800, North York, Ontario M2N 6L9. Tel: 416 512 6569; Toll free: 800 268 9122; Fax: 416 512 6581.

Barbados Tourism Authority, 615 Boulevard Dorchester West, Suite 960, Montreal H3B 1P5. Tel: 514 861 0085; Fax: 514 861 7917.

Addresses in Barbados: Note that all postal addresses should end with 'Barbados, West Indies'.

Barbados Tourism Authority, P O Box 242, Harbour Road, St. Michael, Bridgetown. Tel: 427 2623; Fax: 426 4080. Information desks are also open at the airport and at Bridgetown's harbour.

British High Commission, 147/9 Roebuck Street, P O Box 676c, Bridgetown. Tel: 436 6694.

Canadian High Commission, Bishops Court Hill, Pine Road, St Michael. Tel: 429 3550.

US Consulate, 1st Floor Trident House, Bridgetown. Tel: 436 4950.

Emergencies:

Police – 112. **Fire** – 113. **Ambulance** – 115.

Queen Elizabeth Hospital – Tel: 436 6450.

From Britain, the international dialling code for Barbados is 010-1-809- followed by the local 7-digit number.

From North America, start with 1-809.

From most other Caribbean islands, and within Barbados itself, just dial the 7-digit number.

All the Barbados numbers start with 42 or 43, except for the emergency numbers. All local phone calls are free.

Chapter Five

St Lucia

5.1 Jewel of the Caribbean

St Lucia (pronounced 'Loosha') has been called both the 'Jewel of the Caribbean' and the 'Helen of the West Indies'. It's a beautiful volcanic island with green forests, undulating agricultural land and dazzling beaches.

In this island of contrasts, the visitor can stroll along unspoiled beaches, enjoy the tropical splendour of the interior, marvel at the hot springs in the world's only 'drive-in' volcano, go horse-riding on rugged mountain trails, play golf or simply relax in the sun.

The peaceful Arawak Indians first settled in St Lucia around 200 AD. But some six centuries later they were invaded and replaced by the more war-like Caribs who kept the island to themselves until the early 16th century. The Spanish, Dutch, English and French took turns in trying to take over, but each little settlement was massacred.

Finally the French established themselves around 1650. St Lucia, strategically placed, was equally coveted by the British. Through a complicated 150-year history of battles and treaties, possession of the island changed hands 14 times between the two colonial powers. But for most of that time, French settlers were dominant, with France in possession for nine-tenths of the period from 1651 until 1803.

Hence the island's French flavour – in the place-names, in the patois spoken by the locals, and in the Creole cuisine. Most St Lucians are Roman Catholic.

Like elsewhere in the Caribbean, the Europeans colonised the island to build a plantation economy based on sugar. During that colonisation process, the Carib population faded away, and slaves were imported from Africa. When slavery was abolished in 1834, the plantation owners recruited labourers on contract from India.

The main cash crops were sugar and coconut, but these later were diversified into coffee, cocoa, limes and sea-island cotton. Since 1953, sugar plantations have switched to bananas, which now dominate the island's agriculture. In more recent times, tourism has grown

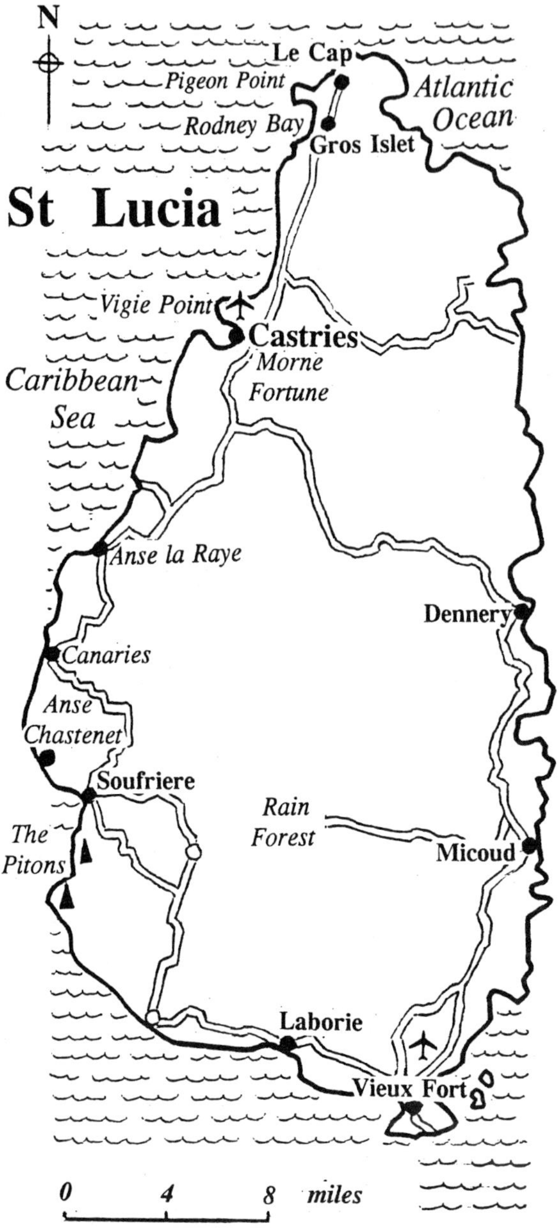
N
Le Cap
Pigeon Point
Atlantic Ocean
Rodney Bay
Gros Islet
St Lucia
Vigie Point
Castries
Morne Fortune
Caribbean Sea
Anse la Raye
Dennery
Canaries
Anse Chastenet
Soufriere
Rain Forest
The Pitons
Micoud
Laborie
Vieux Fort
0
4
8
miles

even more successfully, and currently provides the highest income for the island, bigger than bananas.

Out of the population of some 150,000, roughly one third live in the capital city of Castries. Everybody speaks more-or-less Standard English, besides the local patois. Many St Lucians were running their own businesses by the time independence came in 1967. They are friendly and welcoming to visitors.

St Lucia certainly is paradise-found for those who seek the peace and tranquillity of deserted beaches and sparkling aquamarine bays. The island is a haven for water-sport enthusiasts, with first-class facilities for water-skiing, sailing, wind-surfing and scuba-diving. Whether you simply want to sunbathe while sipping a rum punch, sample the local Creole or international cuisine, or dance the night away to local reggae and steel bands, you'll find all of this and more on St Lucia.

While there is plenty to do and see, St Lucia is essentially a place to relax. St Lucia's great beauty makes it a sought-after destination. Although the island has come into the 20th century, its simplicity and unspoiled nature is a major part of its charm.

During your stay try to hear gospel music in the 19th century cathedral in Castries; see where Dr Doolittle was filmed in the banana plantations above Marigot Bay; ride a horse along the beaches; visit tiny picturesque fishing villages; feast your eyes and nose on the flowers that bloom alongside nearly every road; admire bamboo as tall as houses and even spot a parrot. But that's only if you can spare time away from the gorgeous beaches!

5.2 Arrival & orientation

Long-haul flights from the UK, continental Europe and North America arrive at Hewanorra airport, on the most southerly tip of the island, 38 miles from Castries, the capital.

Alternatively, if you are on a two-centre Island Hopping holiday, your flight may arrive or depart from Vigie airport just outside Castries.

Entry requirements are very simple for visitors from Britain or North America, with just a brief entry form to complete, and no visas required.

Airport procedure is very straightforward. When you come through customs, Thomson clients will be met by the Thomson appointed agent.

A note for the departure: when you leave there is an exit tax of about US $10. But some tour operators like Thomson include that fee in the basic holiday package. If you are leaving from Vigie airport, note that there is no duty-free shop for last-minute purchases.

Most of the larger resort hotels are clustered along the northwest coast, close to Castries. The west coast, facing the Caribbean Sea, boasts quiet secluded coves with clear water and is perfect for watersports. The more rugged east coast is exposed to the more boisterous winds and waves of the Atlantic Ocean.

The island, just 27 miles long by 14 miles wide, lies between the British island of St. Vincent to the south, and the French island of Martinique to the north. The nearest land mass is South America.

The second largest of the Windward Islands, St Lucia offers great scenic variety – lush rain-forests, gentle agricultural valleys, and a mountain range that runs down the centre of the island. The highest peak is Mount Gimie, at 3,117 ft. The dormant Piton volcanoes – greatest sightseeing highlight of St Lucia – are located on the southwestern corner of the island. Effectively it's the western half of St Lucia which offers visitors the most interest.

5.3 At your service

Money and banking: The local currency is the Eastern Caribbean dollar (EC$), divided into 100 cents. It is pegged to the American dollar at $2.70 EC to one US, and fluctuates around $4 EC against sterling. Check local newspapers for the exact exchange rate.

Banking facilities are available in Castries, Rodney Bay Marina, Soufriere and Vieux Fort between 8.00 am and 3.00 pm Monday to Thursday, and until 5.00 pm on Fridays. At Rodney Bay, Barclays Bank and the Royal Bank of Canada are also open on Saturday mornings from 8 am till noon; likewise the Gros Islet branch of National Commercial Bank.

Eastern Caribbean dollars, US and Canadian dollars are accepted by stores, hotels and restaurants, as are travellers cheques and most major credit cards. There's no need to change from US dollar bills to EC dollars, as the US currency is widely used everywhere. Many tourist goods and services are quoted in US dollars. Always make sure there is clear understanding which dollars are being discussed.

Transport: Low-cost minibuses operate along the main routes around the island. The north around Castries and Gros Islet are served very well, and buses run till about 10 pm – or later on Friday nights, when the weekly "jump-up" takes place at Gros Islet. Last bus from Soufriere to Castries leaves at midday. However, many minibuses are driven by speed demons and can be very dangerous. Not recommended!

Plentiful taxis are available. Although unmetered, rates for all standard journeys are fixed by the government. If you wish to hire a taxi for a few hours, or for the day, be sure to negotiate the price in advance. A larger group could hire a minibus as a taxi.

Car hire is another option, though the condition of some of the roads makes driving quite an adventure. From one part of the island to the other, it's sometimes quicker by boat, because of the hilly terrain and delays caused by repair work. Seatbelts should be worn, but are not compulsory. Driving is on the left, more or less, depending on the pot-holes. There's one-way traffic in Castries.

Visitors need a temporary driving permit, obtainable from the local police station – cost around EC$30 (£7.20) – on production of a current driving licence. Car hire costs an average £42 per day. Reckon another £10 a day for insurance.

Electricity: St Lucia operates on 220 volts, 50 cycles, and most hotels are fitted with British 3-pin rectangular plugs. A few hotels have 110 voltage outlets, with US-type plugs. Adaptors are available at all hotels.

5.4 Places to visit

Castries

The St Lucian capital is beautifully situated. Surrounded by hills, its almost landlocked harbour at the head of a wide bay is a constant buzz of activity. Castries is a favourite port of call for cruise ships which dock at Pointe Seraphine; and also a popular stopover for ocean-going yachts and charters. Fishing boats come in at night laden with their catch. Every few days, when banana boats arrive, lorries line up alongside to load St Lucia's main export crop.

The splendid natural harbour has played a key role in St Lucia's history. The ding-dong battles for over 150 years between British and French were aimed around this strategic port. The economic pay-off came later, with the advent of steamships. During a 50-year period from 1880, Castries Harbour was used especially for coal bunkering. Incredibly, around the turn of the century it rated among the world's top twenty ports in volume of freight handled – almost entirely coal, delivered up the gangplank in hundredweight baskets by lines of men and women.

The French laid out the basic grid pattern of the city, but very few colonial buildings remain, owing to bad luck with fires, earthquakes and hurricanes. Most of the buildings are modern, and even the Cathedral dates only from 1894. But this 19th-century Catholic Cathedral is certainly worth a Sunday-morning visit when residents dress up in their Sunday best to participate in the lively art of gospel singing. The colourful interior was specially painted by a local artist, in readiness for a Papal visit in 1986. The same artist – Dunstan St Omer – and his sons also painted the murals at the central bus terminus.

The Cathedral is located on the side of the spacious Columbus Square which in January 1993 was renamed

Derek Walcott Square. Considered to be the finest modern poet and playwright of the English-speaking Caribbean, Derek Walcott was awarded the Nobel Prize for Literature. Derek Walcott is the second Nobel Prize winner from St Lucia, the first being Sir Arthur Lewis – knighted in 1963 – a distinguished economist who has been adviser to many Third World governments.

Something like the Third World is seen every morning at The Market – a large, red iron building constructed in 1894. The busiest market day is Saturday, when the building and the surrounding streets are filled with people selling fresh fruit, spices, vegetables and fish, straw mats, locally crafted baskets and pottery.

Fruit and vegetables range from the commonplace to the exotic, according to season. The familiar potato co-exists with breadfruit, plantain, dasheen, cassava, yam and christophine (a tropical marrow, with a single seed). Tamarinds, soursops, sea grapes, hog plums and sapodillas are displayed alongside familiar High Street sights like lemons, limes, mangoes, melons, bananas, guavas, coconuts, pineapples and avocados. All are used in a wide range of home made pickles, preserves and confectionery. Trying to identify this range of produce can fill an hour, with picture-making of the displays. Caution: in this crowded area, be extra careful with handbag or wallet.

Morne Fortune

Literally meaning 'Good Luck Hill', Morne Fortune offers a stunning panorama over Castries Harbour and Vigie Peninsula, with a sweeping view of the coast from Pigeon Island to the Pitons. The ancient barracks and guard rooms have been restored, and display relics of the British and French forces who fought over St Lucia so many times. A monument to the 27th Foot Royal Inniskilling Fusiliers commemorates a decisive battle in 1796.

Vigie Peninsula

Another lookout point of great military significance during the 18th-century wars between France and England. Today it boasts one of the finest beaches on the island.

South of Castries
Marigot Bay

North of Marigot Bay is the wide Cul-de-Sac valley filled with banana plantations. From above they look like gently moving oceans of green leaves. The Bay itself is rated among the most beautiful in the Caribbean, enhanced by the many sleek yachts at anchor. Marigot Bay is the base of one of the world's largest yacht charter companies, The Moorings.

In 1778, when the British and French were vying for position, Admiral Samuel Barrington, Commander of the British Fleet, evaded the enemy by taking refuge in Marigot Bay and camouflaging his ships as coconut trees by lashing palm fronds to the masts.

Probably this palm-fringed yachtsman's paradise hasn't changed much since then. It was here that the film 'Dr Doolittle' was made in 1966. Animals were shipped in from around the world, while the local inhabitants became 'wild natives' for the filming!

Anse-la-Raye is a vividly coloured fishing village where hand-hollowed canoes are the speciality. 'Anse' is French for Cove, and 'Raye' means Skate.

Soufriere is St. Lucia's second largest settlement, reached through a productive area of citrus, mangoes, breadfruit and tomatoes. During the French-ruled 18th century, Soufriere was the market centre for rich sugar and coffee estates. But in 1780 the city was flattened by a hurricane, and never made a come-back. This deep-water port stands at the foot of two extinct volcanoes, the Pitons. The great depth of the volcanic harbour allows large yachts, cruisers and even freight ships to drop anchor very close to the shore.

The town itself is typically West Indian, a cluster of brightly painted arcaded buildings set hard against the jungle. Some of the older wooden buildings have recently been restored, mainly in the waterfront area.

Rising dramatically from the shoreline, the twin volcanic cones of the Pitons tower over this little town. Petit Piton is 2,461 feet above sea level while Gros Piton reaches 2,619 feet. With their bizarre 60-degree slope, they are probably St Lucia's most famous attraction. The Pitons are essentially the lava core of extinct volcanoes, from which the outer shape has been eroded away for thousands of years.

Although the volcanoes are asleep, the neighbouring **Sulphur Springs** are fully active. These are part of the complex which St Lucians promote as a 'drive-in volcano'. When you have parked, guides conduct you to view the black pits where a witches' brew of bubbling waters belch sulphur fumes. The technical word is a solfatara – a volcanic vent which emits only sulphurous gases and hot mud instead of lava.

Formed by the sulphur springs are the **Diamond Falls**, located a little further down the hillside, in the **Botanical Gardens**, which are themselves worth exploring for beautiful examples of St Lucian plant life. Near the lower falls, with their stunning rock colouration caused by mineral deposits, are the **Diamond Baths** where visitors can bathe in the sulphur enriched water. These hot baths were discovered by the health-conscious 18th-century French, who aimed to develop a Caribbean Aix-les-

Bains. Since restoration of the facilities in 1966, anyone who believes in pungent sulphur fumes and hot water can enjoy the experience.

Rain forest

The road between Soufriere and Fond St Jacques runs through lush rain forest. A number of forest walks can be organised, either through hotels or the St Lucia National Trust. Besides exploring some of the densest rain forest in the Caribbean, visitors can see – if very lucky – St Lucia's indigenous green parrot, one of the most endangered parrot species in the world.

Further south, the picturesque little village of Choiseul is worth a stop for the Arts and Crafts Centre, selling traditional handicrafts. Further along is the fishing village of Laborie.

Moule-a-Chique

Past Hewanorra Airport, the mountainous cape at the southern tip of the island offers a good view of both the Atlantic Ocean and the Caribbean Sea, and as far as the island of St Vincent on a clear day. Here, also, is the world's second highest lighthouse, its rival being in Australia. Ardent bird-watchers could visit the offshore Maria Islands Nature Reserve which is a haven for sea birds and reptiles. But access is not easy. Check arrangements with the Tourist Board.

East Coast Road

The road along the East Coast to and from Hewanorra International Airport has been under reconstruction, with completion scheduled for 1994. This will dramatically improve transfer time to hotels in the Castries area, and will also widen the range of island tours. On the east of the island, dramatic headlands project into the pounding surf of the Atlantic. Swimming is not advisable. Tours to the Fregate Island Nature Reserve are under the wing of the St Lucia National Trust, with frigate birds nesting in summer.

North of Castries

Gros Islet is a traditional fishing village at the northern end of the island. It's best known for holding a street party every Friday night – see the 'Nightlife' section of this chapter.

Pigeon Point is situated just off the village of Gros Islet and was formerly called Pigeon Island. Now the island is joined to the mainland by a causeway, hence the current name of Pigeon Point. It's a superb spot for a picnic.

Pigeon Island was once Admiral Rodney's fortified naval base. From here, Admiral Rodney set sail in 1782 and destroyed the French Fleet at the 'Battle of the Saints' in one of the most decisive engagements in European history. Visitors can wander amongst the historic military ruins, preserved as a National Park.

A small museum is devoted to the island history, with relics in particular of the Carib culture. It also displays specimens of rare St Lucian wildlife.

This end of the island is a blossoming centre for tourism, especially focussed around **Rodney Bay Marina**. Prime sites are available for development, with generous tax holidays and other financial incentives.

Located in the man-made lagoon at Rodney Bay, the marina itself opened in 1986. It houses two charter yacht companies, Stevens Yachts and Tradewinds Yacht Charters Ltd. The area also features "Restaurant Drive" – a collection of excellent local bars and restaurants.

5.5 Take a trip

St Lucia offers some of the Caribbean's most splendid scenery, and is rich in history and culture. It's worth getting around to see more of the island, and meet some of the ever-friendly St Lucian people. Taxi rides work out inexpensive if shared with your fellow hotel guests. Even better are guided tours, with all the details ready organised, door-to-door from all the main hotels. Suggested tours include:

Brig Unicorn Day Cruise

Departing from Castries, a full day's sail aboard a 140-foot square-rigged sloop, down the west coast to Soufriere, which nestles below the twin peaks of the Piton Mountains.

Visit the drive-in volcano, have lunch, and return north with a stop at Anse Cochon for a swim and snorkel, and passing through Marigot Bay where Dr Doolittle was filmed.

Land and Sea: Full Day

For those who want to enjoy the tropical scenery of the west coast road, but who don't want bus-riding all day: drive from Castries to Soufriere, stopping at Morne Fortune before continuing through banana and coconut plantations and past delightful fishing villages to reach Soufriere.

After lunch, return by boat to Castries, with a stop for swimming and snorkelling.

Round the Island: Full Day

This coach tour travels first down the west coast road through plantations and fishing villages to Soufriere. Stops are made at Morne Fortune and the Rum Distillery at Roseau, followed by visits to the Diamond Falls and Sulphur Springs near Soufriere.

After lunch, continue to the southern tip of the island, Moule-a-Chique, where neighbouring St Vincent can be sighted on a clear day. The return journey features the rugged terrain of the east coast, battered by wind and waves of the Atlantic Ocean.

Pigeon Island: Half Day

This tour goes to the northern tip of the island, to scenic Cap Estate, viewing both the Caribbean and Atlantic Sea, followed by sightseeing of Pigeon Island and to the top of Fort Rodney. The guide explains the lifestyle of the early Amerindian settlements, the battles of colonial days, folklore, flora and fauna. There is time for a swim before returning via the little fishing village of Gros Islet.

Marquis Banana Plantation: Full Day

Along the road from Castries to Dennery, a tour of St Lucia's largest working banana plantation begins with a welcome drink served in a coconut. The party then takes a boat trip down the Marquis River, through the heart of the plantation and past mangrove stands rich in birdlife.

The tour shows the original slave quarters and historic buildings, with explanation of how St Lucia's main export crops are produced – banana, coconut and copra; plus the main crops of the past, coffee and cocoa beans. A Creole-style lunch is served on the verandah of the old plantation house.

The Grenadines: Air & Sea

Fly from Vigie airport to Canouan, heading south over St Vincent and the Grenadines, to land at Union Island. Aboard a catamaran, explore some of the numerous islands which form one of the world's most idyllic sailing areas – a popular haunt of wealthy yacht-owners.

Martinique: Day Tour

Fly by chartered aircraft to the French island of Martinique, only 20 minutes away. Stop off at Fort-de-France for a shopping tour with an English-speaking guide. The rest of the day includes an island tour to the village of Saint-Pierre destroyed by the eruption of Mount Pelée in 1902. Passports are required.

Two Day Sailing Cruise to Martinique

Sail to Martinique aboard one of the most modern cruising yachts of the area. Go shopping, sightseeing, swim or just do nothing!

One Day Cruise to Martinique

Cruise from Castries to Fort-de-France – the Paris of the Caribbean. Spend five and a half hours exploring, shopping and sightseeing, before returning to the ship and a welcoming rum punch.

Coastal Excursions

Several boat trips offer an exhilarating day, viewing the island from the sea and possibly weighing anchor to picnic at an exciting location. Means of transport include brigs, catamarans and private yachts.

5.6 All the sports
Watersports

St Lucia is a prime spot for watersports, thanks to strong tradewinds, warm clear water and sheltered anchorages. Many hotels provide facilities for snorkelling, windsurfing and sunfish sailing – often with tuition – at no extra cost to guests.

Arrangements can easily be made for jet and waterskiing, scuba diving and deep sea fishing.

St Lucia is a top-rate location for scuba-diving at the novice level, as the clear shallow water and reefs (only 10 - 20 feet deep) offer an easy approach to the delights of the subaqua world.

For the experienced diver, there is a spectacular drop-off near Soufriere from about 10 to 200 feet. Everything is in reach on a single dive: caves, wrecks, tunnels, schooling fish, eels, massive brain coral and colourful fluorescent sponges.

South of Anse La Raye is a 400-ton freighter – the *Lesleen M* – deliberately sunk in 65 feet of water to create an artificial reef. The wreck is now encrusted with sponges and soft coral, and is the habitat for many species of fish.

Typical costs are £59 for an introductory one-dive course or £59 for two dives for those who hold an international diver's certificate. At Anse Chastanet, a scuba-diving centre can organise five-day diving courses leading to PADI Open Water Certification.

Snorkelling is an excellent alternative to scuba diving for viewing the life and colour of St Lucia's underwater world.

The island abounds in **sailing** and motor-yachting opportunities. Under the bareboat option, you can rent a small sailboat for a few hours, a day or longer, and explore the coastline on your own; or sign up for the crewed option and let your captain do the steering.

For boat charter, try The Moorings in Marigot Bay, or Stevens Yachts or Tradewinds in Rodney Bay.

A number of companies organise **deep sea fishing** trips around St Lucia. Contact your hotel tour desk for further information.

Among the land-based activities, there is a 9-hole **golf course** and **horse riding** at Cap Estate on the northern tip of the island, while all the major hotels have their own tennis courts, many of which are floodlit. Another 9-hole course is located at Sandals La Toc. Non-residents can expect green fees around £7.50 for nine holes, hire of clubs £3.60, and a golf trolley about £1.20.

For those who prefer spectator sport, there's a good chance that local cricket, football or volleyball teams will be in action.

5.7 *Shopping*

Shops are generally open 8.30-12.30 and 13.30-16.00 hrs; Saturday 8.00 till noon. Post office hours are 8.30-16.30 hrs. There are several pharmacies in Castries, and one on the Gros Islet Highway. Most hotels have 'over the counter' type medication such as Aspirin.

Local crafts include ceramics, palm-woven mats and baskets, straw hats, traditional cloth dolls, shells and beads. A good place to buy is at the Saturday morning market in Castries. Pointe Seraphine near the Cruise Ship Harbour has several good duty free shops. Beachwear and T-shirts come in pretty batik and silkscreen designs, often made from sea island cotton. A large selection is available at Bagshaw's, located near to Sandals (formerly La Toc) hotel, south of Castries.

From some hotels there are organised half-day **Shopping Tours** with variable itineraries. But most companies include the colourful fruit and vegetable stalls at Castries market. Following a brief familiarisation tour of the city, you are dropped off to shop to your heart's content! After an allotted time visits may include the Bagshaw's silk-screening workshop, Eudovic Art Studio, Caibelle Batik and St Lucia Perfumes.

For the go-it-alone traveller, here are some suggestions:

Pointe Seraphine (Castries)
The Pointe Seraphine duty-free complex and cruise ship terminal is well worth visiting for its variety of shops that sell local handicrafts, gifts and clothes. Facilities also include restaurants, bars and an information centre. To purchase goods at duty-free prices, visitors must produce their passport and return ticket (sea or air). Purchases can be taken away at the time of sale, except for liquor and tobacco which are delivered to the airport terminal for collection on departure.

Sea Island Cotton Shop (Castries)
Situated on the Morne hill, this shop sells clothes and pictures made from hand-dyed sea island cotton, plus designer T-shirts from 'Kokonuts'.

Bagshaws (La Toc)
Hand-printed silk-screened fabrics that capture scenes from the Caribbean and made into clothes, place mats, wall hangings and bags using Belgian linen. The table linens especially are worth considering. The small workshop is next door, where you can see cloth being printed, and batik work in progress. There's another Bagshaw's branch at Pointe Seraphine.

Noah's Arkade (Castries)
A handicraft and gift shop in the middle of town.

Tapion Craft Ltd (amidst the historic ruins of La Toc)
Straw work, coral jewellery, leather work, coconut and other wood carvings.

Rodney Bay Marina
In addition to all the usual yachting facilities, Rodney Bay Marina has a wide range of shops, including a pharmacy, liquor and stationery stores.

Calabash Gift Shop (Opposite the Sandals Inn, formerly the Halcyon Beach Club)
Offers a selection of paintings by local artists, souvenir items, men's and ladies swim wear, as well as an attractive array of postcards.

La Boutique C17 (Castries)
Situated on Micoud Street, carries a wide range of fashions from Europe and North America, including C17 jeans, beach wear and formal attire.

Pot Pourri (Castries)
Crystal, ceramic picture frames and vases, sunglasses and a wide range of gifts for the family.

Salem Recording Studio (Castries)
Stocks a large range of West Indian music from reggae to calypso. Salem will also record any of your favourite Caribbean music.

Voyager (Castries)
A general retail store specialising in printed T-shirts, dresses and brand name electronic goods and watches.

5.8 Eating out

Thanks to its lush tropical environment, St Lucia is never short of fresh fruits and vegetables, while the seafood was probably caught only a few hours earlier.

Good food flavoured with a French or Creole touch is widely available. Local specialities include lambi (conch), callaloo soup, grilled fresh snapper, crab backs stuffed with spicy crab meat, and baked lobster. Creole dishes are often cooked in a St Lucian coal pot, a type of West Indian hibachi, made of heavy clay and especially suitable for barbecued dishes. A fast-food favourite is roti – meat and potatoes rolled in a pancake.

Fruits include papaya, mango, guava and the many different species of banana. Try some of the wonderful fruit punches, with or without rum. There's a wide range of exotic cocktails that make good thirst-quenchers, in addition to the local beer. But wine and imported spirits are expensive.

Part of the holiday experience is to sample the local cuisine. The major all-inclusive resort hotels concentrate on standard international menus, but they also provide a daily selection of St Lucian dishes. Sample some of these specialities at hotel buffets, where each item is labelled.

For anyone on a room-only package, there is good selection of excellent restaurants up and down the coast. Here's a list suggested by the Tourist Board, but there are many others.

Restaurants in Castries

Le Bamboo, Brazil Shopping Plaza.
(Creole/International) Cosy restaurant serving French Creole cuisine, specialising in coffee and pastries.

Rain, Derek Walcott Square. Tel: 45-23022.
(American and Creole) A green and white building with Somerset Maughan south seas decor inspired by the old movie 'Rain'. A favourite rum punch is a Downpour, which could go with a lunchtime rainburger. The evening speciality is the fixed-price 7-course 'Champagne Dinner of 1885'. The restaurant upstairs features a balcony overlooking the square, and there's a "Pizza Park" under the mango tree in the garden.

San Antoine, Old Morne Road. Tel: 45-24660.
(International) St Lucia's first hotel in the 1920s. San Antoine is a beautifully restored Great House set in 11-acre grounds with spectacular views over Castries Harbour. It offers a sophisticated menu and excellent wine list. Specialities include filet mignon stuffed with crayfish, local fish fillets layered with salmon, and crab and cheese soufflé as an appetiser.

The Green Parrot – Tel: 45-23167.
(International/West Indian) St Lucia's most famous restaurant run by Claridges-trained Chef Harry. Dishes are French and Creole with a distinctive English touch.
Monday, Wednesday and Friday are cabaret nights when Chef Harry takes to the floor himself. Monday night is also Ladies night: if the gentlemen wear jacket and tie, ladies wearing a flower in their hair get a free meal.

Restaurants near Castries

Banana Split, Gros Islet. Tel: 45-28125.
(International/Creole) A completely typical West Indian restaurant – open air and casual – overlooking Pigeon Island. Ideal for a snack before going on to a Friday night street party in Gros Islet. Menu offers boiled lobster, grilled steaks and, of course, banana splits.

D's Restaurant, Edgewater Beach. Tel: 45-37931.
(Creole/International) Dine on the patio, or indoors.

The Plantation House, Bois D'Orange Village. Tel: 45-28213.
(Caribbean) Home-style Creole cooking in the relaxed atmosphere of an old plantation house. Open for lunch and dinner.

Restaurants in Rodney Bay

The Bistro, Rodney Bay. Tel: 45-29494
(Continental and English) Pub fare, lots of pasta dishes, served in a great waterfront atmosphere.

Capone's, opposite St Lucian Hotel. Tel: 45-20284
(Italian) Restaurant and pizza parlour. Interior combines the Jazz age of cops and mobsters of the 1920's and Art Deco touches of the 1930's. Rum drinks include a Valentine's Day Massacre, served by gangster waiters and molls.

Charthouse, opposite St Lucian Hotel. Tel: 45-28115.
(International) Waterfront setting overlooking Rodney Bay, with hickory-smoked ribs, large steaks and lobster in season.

Eagle's Inn, a few minutes' walk from St Lucian Hotel. Tel: 45-20650
(Seafood/West Indian) Creole cuisine in a waterside setting.

Flambée, on Restaurant Drive.
An up-market restaurant with French cuisine.

A-Frame Pub – Tel: 45-28725
Tie up for pub lunch or an evening cocktail. Snacks are served, fish and chips, roti, Mexican chilli.

The Afterdeck – Tel: 45-20665
(International/Creole) Good for sunset drinks overlooking the marina, with seafood and snacks.

Ginger Lily – Tel: 45-28303.
(Cantonese) Hong Kong chefs offer authentic Chinese cuisine at reasonable prices. Take-out available.

The Lime, opposite the St Lucian Hotel. Tel: 45-20761
A popular pub serving local-style grills, roti, and fish lasagne for lunch; seafood to steaks for dinner.

Restaurants in Soufriere & in-between

Doolittle, Marigot Bay. Tel: 45-34246
(International) Simple island food in this wonderful waterside setting. This restaurant was used by the film crew that made the 'Dr. Doolittle' movie in 1966.

The Hummingbird, Soufriere. Tel: 45-47232
(International/West Indian) Dramatic setting, facing the Pitons, with a private pool for use by diners and residents. Delicious Creole menu with crab, lobster and steak. Try the freshwater crayfish in lime and garlic butter.

The Jambette, Anse Jambette. Tel: 45-23167
(International) Owned by Chef Harry of Green Parrot and Claridges fame, with beach barbecues at the weekend.

The Still, Soufriere. Tel: 45-47224
(West Indian/Creole/Seafood) An old rum distillery and plantation house, now serving Creole cuisine using produce of the working plantation itself.

Dasheene, part of the hideaway Hotel Ladera. Tel: 45-47850.
(Creole/Seafood) In a breathtaking location 1,300 feet above sea level between the Pitons, the hotel has won a "Best Chef" award for its Creole and seafood specialities.

Restaurants in Vieux Fort

Chak Chak, near Hewanorra Airport. Tel: 45-46260
(Continental/Creole) Inexpensive West Indian cuisine in a Wild West stockade.

Cloud's Nest – part of the Cloud's Nest Hotel. Tel: 45-46226
(Seafood/Creole)

Il Pirata, on a private beach. Tel: 45-46610
Northern Italian food at reasonable prices.

5.9 Nightlife

There is virtually no nightlife outside the hotels, except for the occasional street party. So the major hotels themselves provide evening entertainment in the form of cabarets, discos, theme nights and folklore shows with steel bands, calypso singers, fire eaters and limbo dancers. Many visitors take a taxi to go hotel-hopping after dark. But do book ahead for restaurants like the Green Parrot and others, which tend to be full every night. At discos, there's a modest admission charge for non-residents, but the reggae is irresistible.

Gros Islet: Evening
This sleepy little fishing village plays host to an impromptu street party of "jump up" every Friday night, when visitors

and St Lucians dance in the streets to reggae and calypso music, and enjoy locally-prepared spicy food, including tasty barbecued chicken. Everyone's welcome to join in the party, with rum and local beer flowing freely, and the evening can get very lively. High-spirited locals will ask women visitors to dance. If they don't want to, the most tactful escape is to say they are married!

Most hotels operate an excursion package, so that you're sure of transport home.

Caribbean Night
Cruise down to Marigot Bay by private motor launch, with cocktails served aboard. Dinner at Marigot Bay and then, after some dancing, the cruise returns to Castries.

5.10 Quick facts

Total area: 238 sq. miles.

Comparative area: 1.5 times the area of the Isle of Wight; 3.5 times the size of Washington, DC.

Coastline: 100 miles.

Natural resources: forests, sandy beaches, minerals (pumice), mineral springs, geothermal potential.

Land use: arable land 8%; permanent crops 20%; meadows and pastures 5%; forest and woodland 13%; other 54%; includes irrigated 2%.

Population: 153,000, growth rate 2.2%.

Life expectancy at birth: 69 years male, 74 years female.

Total fertility rate: 3.5 children born per woman.

Ethnic divisions: African descent 90.3%, mixed 5.5%, East Indian 3.2%, Caucasian 0.8%.

Religion: Roman Catholic 90%, Protestant 7%, Anglican 3%.

Literacy: 67% (male 65%, female 69%).

Labour force: 43,800; agriculture 43.4%, services 38.9%, industry and commerce 17.7%.

Capital: Castries, population 57,000.

Administrative divisions: 11 'quarters' – Anse-la-Raye, Castries, Choiseul, Dauphin, Dennery, Gros-Islet, Laborie, Micoud, Praslin, Soufriere, Vieux-Fort.

Independence: On February 22nd, 1979, St Lucia was granted independence and became a member of the Commonwealth. St Lucia is also a member of the United Nations.

Government: parliamentary democracy.

Legal system: based on English common law.

Executive branch: British monarch, governor general, prime minister, cabinet.

Legislative branch: two-chamber Parliament with an upper house or Senate and a lower house or House of Assembly.

Judicial branch: Eastern Caribbean Supreme Court.

Political parties: United Workers' Party (UWP); Saint Lucia Labor Party (SLP); Progressive Labor Party (PLP).

Suffrage: universal at age 18.

Economy overview: Over the past decade, the economy has shown an impressive average annual growth rate of almost 5% because of strong agricultural and tourist sectors. Saint Lucia also possesses an expanding industrial base supported by foreign investment in manufacturing and other activities, such as in data processing. The economy, however, remains vulnerable because the important agricultural sector is dominated by banana production.

Export commodities: bananas 54%, clothing 17%, cocoa, vegetables, fruits, coconut oil.

Export partners: – UK 51%, Caribbean countries 20%, US 19%.

Import commodities: manufactured goods 23%, machinery and transportation equipment 27%, food and live animals 18%, chemicals 10%, fuels 6%.

Import partners: US 35%, Caribbean countries 16%, UK 15%, Japan 7%, Canada 4%, other 23%.

Industries: tourism, clothing, assembly of electronic components, beverages, lime processing, coconut processing.

Agriculture: accounts for 16% of GDP and 43% of labour force; crops – bananas, coconuts, vegetables, citrus fruit, root crops, cocoa; imports food for the tourist industry.

Fiscal Year: 1 April-31 March.

5.11 Festivals and public holidays

Public holidays that fall on a Sunday are observed on the Monday.

January 1 & 2 – New Year's Day and Holiday
February 22 – Independence Day
Pre-Lent – Carnival celebrations
Easter – Friday, Sunday and Monday
May 1 – Labour Day
May – a 4-day St. Lucian Jazz Festival
Whit Monday – combined with Aqua Action weekend

June 18 – Corpus Christi
June 29 – Feast of St. Peter – Fishermen Day
August 3 – Emancipation Day
August 30 – Feast of St. Rose de Lima
October 5 – Thanksgiving Day
October 17 – Feast of St. Margaret Alacoque
November 22 – St. Cecilia's Day – Feast of the Musicians
December – Atlantic Rally for Cruisers
December 13 – National Day
December 25 & 26 – Christmas and Boxing Days

Carnival St. Lucia

The biggest annual event is Carnival, which explodes two days before Lent. The celebrations with steel bands, dancing and calypso music break loose before dawn on Monday, and continue through Tuesday evening. There is feverish excitement and revelry throughout the island.

Jazz Festival

This major 4-day event was launched in 1992, and is expected to become an annual fixture in the latter half of May. It features a big concert at Pigeon Point Park, and smaller performances at other locations around the island.

Aqua Action

Whitsun weekend is dedicated to an amateur aquatic festival that attracts watersport enthusiasts from throughout North America and the Caribbean. Every imaginable water sport is featured.

Atlantic Rally for Cruisers

The grand finale for a major event in the yachting calendar, when Rodney Bay becomes the finishing point for a trans-Atlantic race.

5.12 Useful addresses

St Lucia Tourist Board, 421a Finchley Road, London NW3 6HJ. Tel: 0171-431-3675; Fax: 0171-431-7920.

High Commission for Eastern Caribbean States, 10 Kensington Court, London W8 5DL. Tel: 0171-937-9522. Open 9.00-17.30 hrs, Mon-Fri.

St Lucia Tourist Board, 9th Floor, 820 2nd Ave., New York, NY 10017. Tel: 212-867-2950; Fax: 212-370-7867.

St Lucia Tourist Board, 4975 Dundas St. W., Suite 457, Etobicoke 'D', Islington, Ontario, M9A 4X4, Canada. Tel: (1)-416-236-0936; Fax: 416-236-0937.

Addresses in St Lucia: Note that all postal addresses below should end with 'St Lucia, West Indies'.

St Lucia Tourist Board, P.O. Box 221, Pointe Seraphine, Castries. Open 8.00-16.30 hrs Mon-Fri. Tel: 45-25968; 30053; 24094. Fax: 45-31121. Information desks are also open at the two airports, and at Soufriere.

British High Commission, 24 Micoud Street, Derek Walcott Square, P O Box 227, Castries. Tel: 45-22484.

French Embassy, Vigie, Castries. Tel: 45-22462.

German Consulate, 6 Manoel St., Castries. Tel: 45-22511.

Medical facilities:

Emergency Tel: 999.

Victoria Hospital, Castries. Tel: 45-22421.

St Jude's, Vieux Fort. Tel: 45-46041.

Soufriere Casualty Tel: 45-97258.

Holiday Agents in St Lucia:

St Lucia Representative Services: Brazil Street, Derek Walcott Square, Box 879, Monrose Building, Corner Brazil-Bourbon St, Castries. Tel: 45-23762/23694/22332; Fax: 45-27922. At Hewanorra Airport, Tel: 45-46175. This company is the local agency for Thomson Holidays.

From Britain, the international dialling code for St Lucia is 010-1-809- followed by the local 7-digit number.

From North America, start with 809.

From most other Caribbean islands, and within St Lucia itself, just dial the 7-digit number, which always begins with 45.

All local 5-digit numbers quoted in older reference books have been converted to 7 digits. The only exception is 999 for emergencies.

Chapter Six

St Kitts & Nevis

6.1 The Columbus connection

Located in the northern part of the Leeward Islands in the eastern Caribbean, the twin islands of St Kitts and Nevis were originally settled by Indians from South America. Christopher Columbus named the islands in 1493, during his second voyage of exploration. The larger island he called St Christopher – not after himself, for he was no saint, but after the patron saint of travellers.

The smaller cloud-capped island reminded Columbus of the snow-capped peaks of Spain, so he named it Our Lady of the Snows – Nuestra Señora de las Nieves. Time and the English gift for language shortened the names to St Kitts and Nevis. But the full official title is the Federation of St Christopher and Nevis.

These two peaceful islands share a stormy past. Ignored by Spanish settlers, the islands were bitterly disputed by France and Britain. Settled by the British in 1623, fighting erupted between the two nations throughout the 17th century, with the added participation of buccaneers, treasure hunters and pirates. The French captured St Kitts in 1666, 1689 and 1782. But the tug-of-war finally ended when Britain gained permanent control in 1783, until Independence came 200 years later. The main reminder of French occupation is in place-names such as Basseterre, Molineux and Cayon.

With the demise of the native Carib population, the growing of sugar was maintained by importing African slaves. The wealth they created led to the building of great plantation houses where the master and his family lived in splendour. Many of these houses fell into ruins when sugar prices collapsed. But some have more recently been restored to economic life as elegant inns or restaurants that cater for luxury tourism.

The islands today offer all the ingredients for a perfect Caribbean holiday: sunshine, watersports, comfortable accommodation and sophisticated cuisine for an international clientele. The keynote is serenity and relaxation.

The blend of African and European traditions is the foundation of the local lifestyle. The people are English-speaking and mainly descended from the early settlers

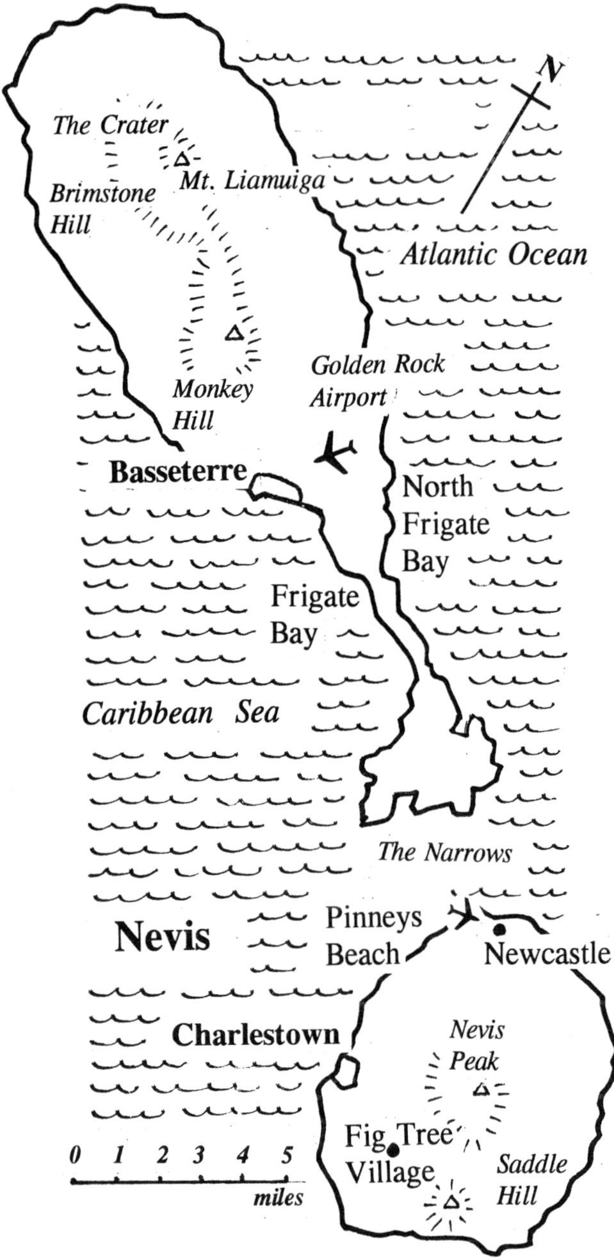
N
The Crater
Mt. Liamuiga
Brimstone
Hill
Atlantic Ocean
Monkey
Hill
Golden Rock
Airport
Basseterre
North
Frigate
Bay
Frigate
Bay
Caribbean Sea
The Narrows
Nevis
Pinneys
Beach
Newcastle
Charlestown
Nevis
Peak
Fig Tree
Village
Saddle
Hill
0 1 2 3 4 5
miles

and slaves. Their friendliness makes the conflict of their ancestry seem light years away. The pace is slow and easy-going, with the locals always ready to take time off for the festivals, parades, cultural shows, calypso dancing and music that reflect the islands' heritage. No matter when you visit, every day will feel like a holiday, in a setting of breathtaking scenery.

The foothills of St Kitts, particularly to the north, form a gently rolling landscape of sugarcane plantations and grassland, while uncultivated lowland slopes are covered with thick tropical woodland and exotic fruits such as mangoes, avocados, breadfruit, bananas and papaya. There are misty mountains, deep ravines, and forests alive with scampering monkeys, a host of birds and a profusion of ferns.

With their near perfect climate, these lush and sleepy islands make you think that maybe the Caribs' original name for St. Kitts was a more descriptive choice. They called it 'Liamuiga: the fertile land'.

6.2 Arrival & orientation

Long-haul flights arrive via Antigua with a half-hour connecting flight by LIAT to Golden Rock Airport on St Kitts.

Upon arrival in St Kitts, you pass through immigration and customs formalities before being met by your tour representative. The agency for Thomson Holidays is Kantours. No visas are required by citizens of Britain, EC, North America and Commonwealth countries.

St Kitts is shaped like a violin upside down. The main holiday hotel developments are in the Frigate Bay area, easily reached from the airport and from the capital city, Basseterre. Golden sandy beaches are located on the north side of the narrow peninsula facing the Atlantic; and on the south side facing the Caribbean. Other beaches around the island are of black volcanic sand.

A recently built highway now reaches to the southern tip of the island, destined for future development. Two miles away, across The Narrows Channel, is the smaller cone-shaped island of **Nevis**, rising to its 3576-ft peak. There are pleasant coral beaches on the island's north and west coasts. Apart from the major golf hotel called Four Seasons Resort, the inns and hotels on Nevis are mostly converted from former plantation houses.

6.3 At your service

Money and banking: The local currency is the Eastern Caribbean Dollar (EC$), divided into 100 cents. Since 1976 it has been pegged at EC$2.70 to one US dollar, and fluctuates around EC$4 against sterling. Check local newspapers for the exact exchange rate. US dollars are widely accepted, and many prices are quoted in both US$ and EC$.

Banking hours are normally 8-15 hrs Monday-Thursday and 8-17 hrs on Friday. Most hotels also exchange currency and travellers cheques, but at less favourable rates. It's better to take US dollars and cheques rather than sterling. Visa is widely accepted by hotels, car hire companies, restaurants and some shops, but Access/Mastercard and Diners Club have more limited acceptance.

Transport
The road system on both islands makes a coastal circuit around the central mountains. Driving is on the left. Privately run bus services make regular but unscheduled runs between villages.

Taxis are readily available and operate on set rates to fixed destinations. Check the tariff before starting your journey. Make sure you have some smaller banknotes, as cabbies rarely have change. If you go out for the evening, arrange to be picked up later. Night fares after 11 pm are surcharged 25%.

Self-drive cars are available, costing £23 to £30 (US$35 to US$45) upwards per day, excluding fuel. A Temporary Driver's Licence must be obtained from the Police Traffic Department, even for motorcycle hire. The cost is EC$30 (£7.50) on presentation of a valid UK driving licence.

Inter-island travel
The regional airline, LIAT, runs five flights daily between Golden Rock airport on St Kitts and Newcastle airport on Nevis. LIAT also operates seven flights a week to and from Antigua, and offers day trip charters to Montserrat, St. Maarten (for duty free shopping), Antigua and Barbuda.

By sea, regular passenger ferry services link Basseterre (St Kitts) and Charlestown (Nevis) with four sailings daily except Thursday and Sunday (travel time 45 minutes). For current timings contact the Port Authority at Basseterre, or the Tourist Office in the Pelican Mall. Cost is approx EC$15 single aboard the privately owned *Spirit of Mt. Nevis*, or EC$10 on the government owned *Carib Queen*.

Electricity is mostly 230 volts 60 cycles AC, although some hotels are on 110 volts. If you bring any electric gadget, choose one with dual voltage, 120/240 volts. Adaptors are available locally, costing EC$20 (£5).

6.4 Places to visit

On St Kitts, the high central body of the island is made up of three groups of rugged volcanic peaks split by deep ravines. The vegetation on the central mountain range is rain forest, thinning higher up to dense bushy cover. The island's volcanic crater, Mt Liamuiga, rises to almost 4,000 ft. The southeast of the island is a low-lying peninsula, with excellent beaches.

Basseterre is the island capital, with quaint examples of Georgian and French colonial architecture. The Circus with its clock tower and surrounding 'gingerbread' buildings is the best starting point for sightseeing and shopping. Worth a photo are the Government House and many Georgian buildings around Independence Square. Basseterre's deep water port is regularly visited by cruise liners operated by Cunard, Sun Line, Home Line and several others.

For history buffs, **Brimstone Hill** is a vast limestone rock rising over 700 feet high, nestling under the gentle slope of Mount Liamuiga. Built in 1690, this 'Gibraltar of the West Indies' was the scene of several Franco-British battles during the 18th century. Here, first the British and later the French commanded a garrison. You can drive almost to the summit for magnificent views over Statia, Saba and other nearby islands in the Leeward chain. Now partly reconstructed and with its guns remounted, Brimstone Hill was opened by the Queen as a National Park in 1985.

Nevis

The conical island of Nevis rises to the central peak of 3576-ft Mt Nevis. The mountain is flanked on the north and south sides by two lesser mountains, Saddle Hill and Hurricane Hill, which once served as look-out posts for Nelson's fleet. On the island's west side, palm trees form a coconut forest. The island is skirted by miles of silver sand beaches and a calm, turquoise sea in which great brown pelicans dive for fish.

The capital, **Charlestown**, is a delightful town. Weathered wooden houses are covered with bougainvillaea. A typical Caribbean market is open weekdays. Visit the cotton ginnery, the old mineral baths on the edge of town and the museum birthplace of the American statesman Alexander Hamilton.

Of more interest to British visitors is the Nelsonian Museum in Charlestown. During 1787 young Nelson was stationed in Nevis as commander of the *Boreas* frigate. At St John's Church in **Fig Tree Village**, the register records the marriage of Horatio Nelson to a local widow, Fanny Nisbet. The best man was the Duke of Clarence, who later became William IV. The wedding was held on the sugar plantation where the Montpellier Inn is located.

North of Charlestown is **Pinney's Beach**, one of the best on the island, an expanse of silver sand backed by rustling palms. Further north still, Black Sand Beach and Hurricane Hill offer excellent views. Other beaches to explore include Nisbet beach and Oualie beach which possess good watersport facilities including scuba diving.

6.5 Take a trip around St Kitts

To explore the islands, there is good choice of excursions which can be arranged through Kantours. Ask your rep for details and prices.

For the energetic, a **Rain Forest Hike** is a fascinating choice. A favourite circuit goes by Land Rover to the base of a trail, followed by a scenic $1^1/_2$ hour walk to Lawyer Stevens Cave', with time to admire the flora and fauna en route.

More strenous is a spectacular **Volcano Tour** – *not recommended for children, the elderly or those suffering from asthma or heart ailments.* After a $1^1/_2$ hour Land Rover journey, the hike through the rain forest to the crater rim takes about $2^1/_2$ hours. Stops for breath give a chance to learn from your guide about the flora and fauna. The return to base is normally faster. Wear suitable shoes, long trousers and take a sweater – it's cold on top!

Focussing on the island's sugar and coffee industries, a **Plantation Tour** takes you through cane fields to a romantic Great House where an elegant creole lunch is served. Experience the lifestyle of the former landowners!

An all-day **Island Tour** goes around the scenic coast with several stops, including a visit to Brimstone Hill. The Great House of Romney Manor doubles as a centre for high-grade batik, produced amid stunning surroundings. Old Road Village was the landing point of the first English colonist, Sir Thomas Warner.

There are several day cruise options, with stops at secluded beaches for swimming, snorkelling and a barbecue lunch. Sunset cruises with an open bar are a popular choice.

Day trips around Nevis include the main highlights already mentioned in the previous section.

6.6 All the sports

Swimming is excellent, either in hotel pools, or from the choice of Atlantic or Caribbean sandy beaches. Facilities are good for all the popular watersports, including windsurfing, waterskiing and sailing. Deep sea fishing trips are a speciality, costing around £40 per person, beer and tackle included.

In the crystal clear waters there is great pleasure in snorkelling and scuba diving, with coral reefs and some old shipwrecks to explore. Major resort hotels offer professional instruction.

Golf: The Royal St. Kitts at Frigate Bay (close to Sun 'n' Sand and Jack Tar Village) is an 18-hole international championship course. There's also a nine-hole course at Golden Rock.

For the ultra-keen golfer, an 18-hole palmtree-lined course designed by Robert Trent Jones II is attached to the Four Seasons Resort on Nevis (Tel: 469 1111).

Tennis: Numerous courts are available on both islands, and clubs welcome visitors. Many hotels have their own (mainly hard) tennis courts.

Other land-based activities include mountaineering, hiking, cricket, football and horseriding.

6.7 *Shopping*

Shops are open weekdays 8-12 and 13-16 hrs, but some stay closed on Thursday and Saturday afternoons.

Local handicrafts include carvings, baskets, straw and coconut work. Hand printed T-shirts, scarves and beach cover-ups are also very popular. Caribelle Batik Factory at Romney Manor is considered to be the world's most beautiful factory, set amid five acres of lush tropical gardens. Craftsmen produce colourful batik garments and wall hangings that are exported throughout the Caribbean.

There are several Duty Free gift shops and a shopping mall in Basseterre. However, duty-free shopping is relatively new to St Kitts and only a few shops feature imported merchandise at worthwhile savings.

Post Offices are open daily 8-15 hrs, except Thursday 8-11 hrs. Airmail to UK takes 5-7 days.

There are two local newspapers – the weekly *Democrat* and the twice weekly *Labour Spokesman*.

6.8 *Eating out*

Most restaurants offer international menus with island variations. Local dishes include roast suckling pig, spiny lobster, turtle steak, lemon grass chicken, crab back or curries. Freshly caught seafood is plentiful. Restaurants that cater more for locals also offer pumpkin soup, conch (curried, soused or in salad), turtle stews, rice and peas and goat's water (mutton stew). Snackbars serve pizzas, hamburgers and barbecue grills.

Many restaurants, especially those in the old plantation houses, grow their own vegetables and fruit: pumpkin, aubergine, breadfruit, plantain, mango and christophene, served according to season.

Imported drinks are available. Try the excellent Cavalier rum from Antigua, or the locally brewed Carib beer.

6.9 Nightlife

On both islands, nightlife is low key. Some hotels and inns have string or steel bands for Saturday night dancing in the peak season of mid-December to February. Jack Tar Village at Frigate Bay has a casino, complete with slots, roulette and blackjack. Otherwise entertainment centres around the pleasant bars, with sometimes a disco. See below in section 6.10 for details of Carnival on St Kitts, and a Cultural Festival on Nevis.

6.10 Festivals and public holidays

The basic public holidays are:
Jan 1 – New Year's Day; Easter Friday and Monday; May 1 – Labour Day; Whit Monday; 2nd Saturday in June – Queen's Birthday; 1st Monday in Aug – Emancipation Day; Sep 19 – Independence Day; Christmas and Boxing Day.

Carnival

During the Christmas and New Year festive season, a week-long Carnival is held in St Kitts with masquerades, street dancing, calypso competitions and cultural shows, besides the usual Christmas dances and celebrations. Visitors are encouraged to join in.

Nevis celebrates a Culturama in late July/early August, with cultural shows, calypso and talent contests, parades, dancing and street jamming.

6.11 Useful addresses

St Kitts & Nevis Tourist Board, 10 Kensington Court, London W8 5DL. Tel: 0171-376-0881. Fax: 0171-937-3611.

High Commission for Eastern Caribbean States, 10 Kensington Court, London W8 5DL. Tel: 0171-937-9522. Open 9.00-17.30 hrs, Mon-Fri.

St Kitts & Nevis Tourist Board, 414 East 75th Street, New York, NY 10021. Tel: (212)-535-1234. Fax: (212)-734-6511.

Consulate of the Federation of St Christopher and Nevis, 2501 M Street NW, Washington DC 20037. Tel: (202)-833-3550.

St Kitts and Nevis Tourist Board, Pelican Mall, Bay Road, P O Box 132, Basseterre, St Kitts. Tel: 465 2620.

or Main Street, Charlestown, Nevis. Tel: 469 1042.

British High Commission in Antigua deals with enquiries relating to St Kitts and Nevis.

Chapter Seven

Cash crops and fruit

For garden-lovers there's great pleasure in touring through the countryside, and seeing first-hand how the tropical crops, fruits and vegetables are grown.

Plantation crops on one or more of the islands include sugar cane, coffee, cocoa, rice, coconuts and bananas. Smaller farms and backyard plots produce maize, beans, onions, sweet potatoes and other tubers for domestic consumption and local market sale. But land is being reallocated for increased production of non-traditional export crops such as winter vegetables and exotic fruits. You can see avocado trees, mangoes, papayas, passion fruit, citrus, peanuts and cashews.

Here are some background notes.

Sugar

Ever since Christopher Columbus brought sugar cane to the Caribbean in 1493, sugar has played a dominant role in the island economies. For centuries there was fast-expanding world demand for the end product, bringing riches to estate owners. The annual consumption of sugar in Europe rose from 5 lbs per person in 1700 to more than 90 lbs in the 1930's.

Sugar cane is harvested once a year, usually starting around mid-May when the cane is anything from 4 to 10 feet tall. Cutting is done by hand, with machetes, no machinery. It's very tough labour-intensive work.

When the cane is cut, new shoots arise from the stubble, growing up ready for next year.

Historically, the planters' need for labour was met by the import of slaves.

This was the basis of the 'Devil's Triangle' pattern of trade: sugar and rum sold to Europe bought consumer goods to exchange for West African slaves who were sold in the Caribbean – with big profits along each side of the triangle. When slavery was abolished, some planters recruited contract labour from the Indian sub-continent.

Sugar production remains important, though St. Lucia has switched mainly to bananas and cacao which are less labour-intensive; and Antigua has given up, to specialise in pineapples. Barbados is still deeply into sugar. A by-product is molasses, which is fermented to meet the local and international demand for Barbados rum. An acre of good land can produce ten tons of cane which converts into a ton of sugar, with thirty gallons of rum as a bonus from the molasses.

An estimated one thousand rum shops are the main social centres for the average male Bajan, and the same model is followed in other Caribbean islands.

Bananas

Shortly after the arrival of Columbus, banana trees were introduced from the Canary Islands into Hispaniola. From there, the trees spread throughout the Caribbean and to Central and South America – to all the latter-day banana republics.

A banana plantation provides year-round fruit. Bananas grow well, almost anywhere on the lushly fertile islands, and are also a backyard crop for domestic consumption. A close relative is the plantain, looking like a large green banana, and cooked as a vegetable. Banana exports go mostly to USA, but also to Britain.

The plant is hermaphrodite: male and female flowers on the same stalk. Reproduction takes place without pollination. The first flowers appear when the plant is about one year old. Bananas are the female part of the flower, and at the tip of the flower stalk is the male organ. Each row of bananas is separated by large purple bracts, or petals, which are cut off by hand to expose the bananas to the sun.

The bananas gradually turn upwards, and fatten. The stem is cut green for export at six or seven months. After removal of the fruit, the thick fibrous stems are used as fodder. The original plant dies, but is replaced by suckers.

Coconuts

Thousands of coconut palms flourish mainly in coastal areas. As a commercial crop, the tree is cultivated mainly for oil extracted from the dried copra. Crude oil is an ingredient in soap and cosmetics, while refined oil is used for cooking, and for manufacture of margarine and salad oils. Coconut milk can double as a suntan lotion, and plays a key role in piña coladas.

Wayside vendors offer fresh coconut milk, scalping the fruit with a machete. Some islanders claim that coconut juice is an aphrodisiac, though that may be just a sales pitch. People who stop for a drink also own the flesh of the coconut. But usually they don't bother, just leaving it with the street vendor.

By-products help rank the coconut palm among the world's most useful trees. The outer casing makes good fertilizer, while the very strong coir fibre is used for rope-making, coarse brushes and matting. The second shell burns well as fuel. Palm leaves make an economy thatch.

Coconuts are disseminated by independent sea travel. The fibrous husk keeps the fruit afloat, while the tough skin prevents water-logging. Swept by tides and currents onto a distant shore, the nut germinates rapidly, even after four months' afloat.

Growing 100 feet tall, coconut palms begin to yield after six years, and remain productive for a century. If a fruit is harvested green from four months onwards, it contains mostly sweet milk. Otherwise the fruit takes a year to ripen, when the milk has become solid and oily to produce the coconut meat. An average tree bears over 40 nuts annually, yielding about 20 lbs of copra from which a gallon of oil can be extracted.

Cacao

The cacao tree produces the totally different bean from which cocoa and chocolate are made. Grown in St. Lucia, the 25-ft evergreen trees produce large red pods, each containing about 50 bitter-tasting beans. These seeds, weighing about 200 to the pound, are dried in the sun for three days. Then they are roasted and ground for cocoa and chocolate manufacture.

Chapter Eight

Caribbean eating and drinking

The major hotels and restaurants concentrate on standard international cuisine. But mostly they also provide a daily selection of local dishes. Traditional Caribbean cuisine is worth trying. It's a mixture of the ethnic influences that have created each island's identity: a savory yet subtle blend of British, (French in St Lucia), African and Asian.

You can sample some of these specialities at hotel buffet meals, where a label with the local name is attached to each food item on display. But more cautious palates will find that grills, steaks, hamburgers and the like are also well represented on dining room menus.

Caribbean cooking is traditionally robust, tasty and filling to satisfy people whose lives involved hard physical work to support large families on a tight budget. Imaginative spicing added variety to a limited range of staples. Dishes rooted in the islands' past still form the basis of most people's daily meals.

Herbs and spices are grown all over the islands, adding their own aromatic scent to the air. Hot, tangy and sour tastes are popular. Garlic, chillies, red and green peppers, onions, shallots, thyme, cloves, nutmeg and limes are widely grown and used with abandon. Town dwellers still buy much of their produce at street markets rather than supermarkets, and make their own preserves and pickles.

Fish is plentiful, and can appear in many styles of cooking. Flying fish, red snapper, dolphin fish, swordfish, tuna, lobster and shrimp are all found in waters around the islands.

The Caribbean choice of meat is more limited, with pork and poultry and possibly goat as the traditional mainstays. The available meat is stretched by using it more as a flavouring to the rice and vegetables. Peas or beans and rice especially are used as a main dish, seasoned with whatever meat is available.

One of the Caribbean's most popular dishes is "pepperpot" – an everlasting casserole of meats and peppers, which gets its distinctive flavour and longevity from cassareep, a juice derived from cassava, the root crop originally grown by the Arawak Indians. Like a stockpot, it can be kept going for months on end.

The 20th century has brought a wider variety of foods to the islands, including the hamburger and the pizza. But despite the convenience of pre-prepared foods, the majority of island families remain faithful to their own traditional, well-loved cuisine.

All the fruits

The islands harvest a year-round choice of tropical fruits. Bananas, pineapples, coconuts, melons and watermelons, oranges, lemons, grapefruit, mangoes and limes are familiar enough. But there are many other fruits which are more difficult to recognise by visitors from North America or Europe.

Especially delicious is passion fruit, which makes an excellent drink or is superb with a scrape of honey. Papaya or paw-paw is a good breakfast starter, with a twitch of lemon or lime juice to enliven its otherwise bland flavour. Guava provides excellent fruit juice, and can be converted into marmalade. Sapodilla is a rough-skinned fruit like a plum, used in ice cream and milk shakes.

Among other fruits that appear in farmers' markets are tamarind, medlar, and custard apple. Another fruit worth trying is the mamey – size of a grapefruit with brown skin and sweet orange-red pulp which can be eaten raw or cooked.

All the drinks

Combinations of fresh fruit juices are ubiquitous, and coconut water from fresh green coconuts is sold on every street corner.

However, rum is undoubtedly the king of the West Indies. Rum is used to create a huge variety of cocktails and punches, often in combination with fresh fruit juices, as well as drinking it neat. Distilleries produce blends of different age and strength for the connoisseur.

The standard product can be found at rum shops, an all-male preserve with many similarities to the English pub. To visit the West Indies without tasting the rum is like visiting Scotland without sampling the malt whisky.

Rum cocktails

Caribbean ingenuity has devised many ways of absorbing the fruit, sugar and rum mountains. Here are some popular variations, with the exact proportions and ingredients depending on the barman.

Piña Colada – white rum, pineapple juice, lemon juice, cream of coconut and ice.

Rum punch – rum, lime juice, sugar syrup, soda water and ice; plus a twitch of nutmeg, some mint and five drops of bitters.

Planter's punch – same as a rum punch, but decorated with chunks of fruit.

Fruit punch – rum, different fruit juices, soda and ice (also possible without the rum).

Daiquiri – white rum, lemon juice, sugar and ice.

Banana-daiquiri – as for daiquiri, but with banana and orange juice.

Rum cocktail – rum, gin, lemon juice, sugar and ice.

Cuba libre – a famous calypso gives you the ingredients: rum and Coca-Cola.

Wines
The islands do not have any significant wine production. Many table wines are imported from Chile, Spain or California. Quality European wines and champagnes are on the wine-lists of top-grade restaurants. But – to the distress of wine-lovers – they are much more expensive than in their countries of origin.

Chapter Nine

Travel Tips

9.1 Tipping

Hotel and restaurant bills usually include a 10% service charge. For exceptional service, a few more dollars would be appropriate – as at any other upmarket location, but at your discretion. A small tip is usual for porters – say, the equivalent of 50 US cents per bag – whilst 10% is normal for cabbies. Maids are tipped according to service, say the equivalent of US$1 per day. Depending on the circumstances, tipping always helps to smooth the way but the islanders are not avaricious. Tipping is not always necessary at 'all-inclusive' hotels.

9.2 East Caribbean time

The eastern Caribbean islands are on Atlantic Standard Time, 4 hours behind GMT, and don't alter clocks for summer. Thus, during Britain's 'summer time', April to October, the islands are 5 hours behind UK. October to April, they are 4 hours behind British Time.

They are the same as Eastern Standard Time in New York and Miami during America's daylight saving months; otherwise, one hour ahead for the rest of the year.

The hour of sunset varies very little, year-round, about 7.30 p.m., with brief twilight.

Caribbean islanders have a laid-back view about time, and don't take punctuality too seriously.

9.3 Phoning home

Think twice before phoning home from your hotel. A standard 3-minute minimum call to UK can be quite expensive. Carefully check the rules. In theory, the computer system shouldn't start counting your time until you get a response from the number you are dialling. But some hotels advise that you shouldn't let the phone make more than five rings. Otherwise a minimum 3-minute charge is automatically charged to your account.

To call Britain dial 011-44 for UK, omit the zero of the STD code and continue to dial as normal. Don't forget the 4- or 5-hour time difference.

For North America, dial the US or Canadian area code plus the number required.

If there is a phone in your room then either you can dial direct, or the hotel operator will make the connection and call you back. If the hotel has no phones in the rooms, calls can be made from reception. It is sometimes necessary to wait for an international line so do not expect to get a call instantly. International calls are handled by Cable and Wireless.

Here are the approximate costings of phone calls to Europe. But remember that individual hotels apply different mark-ups.

Antigua Reckon £5.28 for the first 3 minutes plus £1 for each further minute. There is a 20% government tax on all overseas calls.

Barbados Expect to pay £5.50 for any part of 3 minutes plus £1 – £2 for each further minute.

St Lucia Rates are approx £1.50 per minute. A cheaper rate applies between 6 pm and 6 am, costing approximately £1.15 per minute.

St Kitts Minimum £1 per minute.

9.4 News

Each of the islands has at least one newspaper, while weekly or monthly tourist publications are a useful source of information for local events. In Barbados, for instance, there are two dailies – *The Advocate* and *The Nation*; and two Sunday papers. The tourist newspapers are free – *The Visitor*, weekly; and *Sunseeker*, fortnightly.

Magazines and newspapers such as the 'Miami Herald', 'The Wall Street Journal', 'International Herald Tribune', 'Financial Times' (US edition), 'Newsweek' and 'Time' are available a day or two after publication. Sometimes you can find London newspapers, with the price heavily loaded by the cost of air travel.

Television – Most hotel satellite TV's give you local programmes, news by courtesy of CNN, and other channels from America's deep south. The visitor from Britain can feel cut off from UK-flavoured news.

It's worth travelling with a short-wave radio, to pick up the regular on-the-hour news bulletins of the BBC World Service. Reception varies according to time and location, and can always be improved if you take a length of aerial wire to dangle from your hotel window. Try the following wave-lengths:

Morning 7.00-10.00 hrs – 15220 kHz on 19-metre band; 6195 kHz on 49m band.
Day-time 10.00-12.15 hrs – 17840 kHz on 16m band.
Evening 18.00-00.30 hrs – 9915 kHz on 31-metre band; 7325 on 41m band; 5975 kHz on 49m band (from 16 hrs).

9.5 Security

The eastern Caribbean islands are low-risk for holiday-makers and their valuables. But – like anywhere in the world - occasional break-ins can happen, though they are rare in the all-inclusive hotels which control entry at the perimeter gate. It's good policy to put your credit cards, travellers cheques, jewelry, passport and return ticket into safe deposit. Many hotels have a room safe at a small charge.

Outdoors, just like in any other country, take particular care of handbags and wallets in crowded areas such as markets. In the evening, ensure that a handbag has nothing of value in it. Late at night it's preferable to use a taxi and avoid carrying large wads of money.

If you have the misfortune to experience any sort of crime, report it to your hotel, who will contact the police as necessary. An official loss report is needed for any insurance claim.

Regardless of your destination, it's always a wise precaution to keep a separate note of traveller-cheque and credit card numbers, together with the hot-line telephone to ring in case of loss.

9.6 Photo hints

In the brilliant Caribbean sunshine, slowish films around ASA 100 will give good results for colour prints. Concentrate your picture-making on early morning or late afternoon. Noontime sun makes people squint, and the strong light on beaches casts very harsh shadows. Also, the midday sun gives too much glare, though a lens hood and a polarization filter can help overcome the problem.

Towards evening, dusk is of short duration. Capture that sunset picture quickly, before it disappears! Make your beach photos more interesting with a foreground tree as a frame or silhouette.

Fine sand on the lens can be a nuisance. Keep the lens cap in place, whenever the camera is not in use. Bring some lens-cleaning tissue and a dust brush. To protect the lens, it's worth leaving a skylight filter permanently in place - much less costly to renew if over-vigorous cleaning causes scratches. Don't leave your camera lying in the sun, as heat can harm the film.

In the principal tourist locations, local people are accustomed to visiting shutterbugs with their desire to point cameras in every direction. Elsewhere, folk may be less tolerant of any invasion of their privacy. Ask permission before taking anyone's photo. This will probably be given quite cheerfully, especially if a few coins change hands.

However, if you don't make a big production of it, you can still get colourful shots of people in characteristic activity. Position yourself by a monument or in a crowded market, or at a crossroads. With a wide-angle lens for close-up, or long-focus lens for more distant shots, you can discreetly get all your local-colour pictures without irritating anyone.

Take flash for pictures of evening activities and entertainments – but photography in casinos is not allowed.

Film prices are much higher than in Britain or USA, so take plenty. If you use a specialised film, rather than standard brands, then take an over-supply. Off-beat films are hard to find. For cameras that use batteries, be sure to replace them before travelling on holiday – or pack a spare set.

Keep a note of photos taken, and their sequence. Otherwise, back home, it's very difficult to identify every picture. In postcard size, one beach can look remarkably like another.